DJ DIARIES

DAVE DONAHUE
DJ DIARIES
RADIOS REMARKABLE LISTENERS

VOLUME ONE

DJ DIARIES
RADIO'S REMARKABLE LISTENERS

Author Photo credit: Ken Gagne

iUniverse books may be ordered through booksellers or by contacting:

iUniverse
1663 Liberty Drive
Bloomington, IN 47403
www.iuniverse.com
1-800-Authors (1-800-288-4677)

ISBN: 978-1-5320-0880-1 (sc)
ISBN: 978-1-5320-0879-5 (e)

Library of Congress Control Number: 2016919907

Print information available on the last page.

iUniverse rev. date: 12/28/2016

To Disk Jockeys world-wide, those on-the-air personalities all across the radio dial everywhere and their listener's that have shared their remarkable stories within this book. We thank you.

Other volumes of the DJ Diaries are in production. If you are a DJ or listener that wants to add a story, please visit our website.

davedonahue.net

No real person's names or locations will be published due to the nature of some of the stories. All mail will be considered confidential and will be secured in a safe at another address.

Contents

Prologue: "Testing ... testing!"

* (S peech delivered by author at various functions across the nation.)

**"Testing—one—two—three ...
Hello? May I have your attention, please?"**

I've talked to you countless times over the years and you have reacted to my conversations in various ways. Now for the first time, I'm truly excited about having the opportunity to converse with you through the pages of this book ...

Don't remember me, huh?

I sure remember you. In fact, I bet as you read this book you'll vaguely recall some of my conversations. Let me refresh your memory.

Truth is, the other morning I woke you up, talked to you while you were in the bathroom, and even updated you on the world affairs while you tried to match your socks.

Then I guided you through a quickie breakfast, urging you to have another cup of coffee before you tackled the traffic jam ahead and the jam you'd be in if you were late for work.

You know, I can't recall the numerous times I reminded you that the weather was going to dump buckets of water on your head by afternoon. Because you forgot your umbrella, you cussed me out and it wasn't even my fault. I told you about the rainy weather earlier, while you were still trying to locate your mouth with a cup of coffee. Remember?

Okay, now brace yourself. There is something that's not going to be easy telling you about but—here goes.

While you were off at work breaking your back to make a buck, I sneaked back into your house and had an affair with the little lady!

Yes, it's true. It has happened countless times.

I've told her about the latest fashions, where to shop, what to buy with your money and have even suggested that life could be a little more pleasant if she would run off with the next person that rings your doorbell.

Then by late afternoon while you bumped you way home through the savage snarls of traffic, I've patted you on the ears and did my best to sooth the *"beast within"* that sprung up during the day at the office. You know, I seem to recall you mumbled all the way home, but I did get a little smile or two out of you before you pulled up in the driveway. You are going to tell your wife that funny I told you that you giggled over.

Hey! I've entertained your kids—even been a baby sitter with them when you're away from home in the evenings.

Also, I've been up with you some pretty late hours when you felt lonely and did my best to help fill up that empty room.

We've been to the beach together and I've followed you and other fans to countless football, basketball and baseballs games. You sure count on me to have the latest scores, don't you?

I have made you laugh, smile, giggle, smirk, get angry, tap your foot—even cry.

Oh, I really, really hope I don't embarrass you when I tell you that I've shared in some of your most sensual and intimate moments. Oh ... and you thought everyone was asleep, right?

Yes, I have even made friends with some of your friends, but they tell me that they take me for granted more often that not. Some claim they don't ever hear what I say. Yet, they can recall nearly everything I said earlier when and if ... it benefits their needs.

I've been nearly everywhere you've been and then some. I've been to the North Pole and the moon and back—even put some time in on the bottom of the ocean in a submarine.

Who am I?

I am a twenty-four-hour-a-day, seven-day-a-week-come-rain-or-shine-happy-go-lucky-burst-of-everything-you-need-to-know-BABBLE-IN-A-BOX!

I am **THAT VOICE** you hear **ON THE RADIO.**

True, it is almost beyond reality that I am crammed into that thin box of wires and electronic circuit boards called a radio. I am streaming in your phone, your computer, even in some showers! Sure, you may never see me or meet me, but I do have a body and a mind and I breathe air and walk the land just like you.

I AM A DISK JOCKEY!

It has always been fascinating to listen in on the conversations between listeners and disc jockeys when the listener ventures into the vast, complex work world of the DJ. The listener is always amazed at the *'control room.'*

Many first time visitors compare it to seeing the cockpit of an airliner.

We the DJ's can explain the knobs, dials, switches, buttons, meters, lights and buzzers easy enough, but if you gaze into the eyes of the visiting listener you most often see total bewilderment.

I think most of them picture us in their mind as sitting in a chair, feet propped up, talking into a microphone. No, not even close. It's more like flying that airliner.

"Golly ... wow, this is really something. You go to school or something to learn all this stuff?" the listener says, trying to take in the darkened room with the speakers on the wall blaring, and the jock swiveling in his chair, arms and hands flying everywhere.

Nope," the disc jockey replied, keeping his eyes on the blinking lights and meters, "I just sort of hung around a radio studio like this one, ran errands, swept the studios and pestered them until they let me go on the air and read the weather one day. Been at it ever since.

"Must be fun playing all those songs and stuff?"

"Yeah, it's an okay job, wait, hold on ..." The DJ puts on his earphones, punches a couple of buttons and speaks into the microphone in front of him. When he's through he turns to the visitor again.

"That was neat. Boy, I'd sure like to have your job," the visitor is impressed. "Bet is sure pays good, huh?"

"Yeah, sometimes, let me ask you a question. What do you do?"

"Me? Heck, all I do is put five bolts on a car fender down at the auto plant."

"You made about what last year—fifty or sixty thousand, maybe more?" The DJ grins.

"Uh, it's somewhat around that."

"Also you work a five day work week, and I'd say with seniority at the plant you more than likely get all the best shifts, holidays off and about a month's vacation on top of that to boot, right?

"True. But ..." the visitor starts as he shifts uncomfortably from foot to foot.

"You get overtime and time and a half or even double time pay on holidays and about fifty so percent of your paycheck when the company goes on a strike, plus welfare, true?"

"Uh, sure doesn't everybody," the visitor answers somewhat defensively.

"You got a wife, about two kids, a nice home, a boat, a camper and about six credit cards?"

"The hell you say. How'd you guess about all that?"

"Wasn't hard really, we have surveys and ratings that tell us about our average listeners. That's you my friend."

"Damn, say ... uh, I bet you get a lot of calls from sexy women?" the visitor snickers, trying to change the subject.

"Sure, lots of people out there. Say, want to trade jobs? Come on, sit right down here behind the ole microphone and—"

"Oh crap man, are you crazy!" The visitor looks around in a panic unsure of himself. "I don't know what to do, and I ... don't know what to say and, and ..."

"Okay relax, here's how being a DJ really is."

"The average DJ's life-span in radio is about five years. If the DJ is lucky by that time he might have only moved two or three times to finally pump his pay check up to about $500 dollars a week if he's lucky! The jock does countless personal appearances which usually are not paid for because radio stations call it 'publicity' which is what you do to have good enough ratings to keep your job. The word 'holiday' doesn't exist and neither does 'overtime' pay at most small radio stations. On top of that, DJ's work some of the strangest hours ever. They will sometimes answer about two hundred incoming telephone calls a shift and always have the pressure of the fact that the boss could be listening at any time.

Also, everything a DJ owns must fit into a small trailer because at the slightest dip in their ratings another up and coming air talent (who will usually work for less pay) will get their job."

(Oh, say ... if you have ever been replaced while on vacation raise your hand. (*It's hard for me to type with one hand!*)

"Sadly," the DJ continues, "a lot of DJ's are usually divorced a couple of times because of working such odd hours, and with the low pay, no holidays, and lack of stability due to the radio rating game, it's tough luck, so try again.

It also means many can't qualify for credit cards, home loans and so on.

Finally, have you noticed how most of the disc jockeys on the air today in every town and city, sound like they have underdeveloped voices like high school kids? Most sound alike and not many sound real, big, booming, resonant, pleasant, sincere or unique.

DJ's with that one-of-a-kind, I mean 'I-am-man kind voice, and great personalities are considered 'old school' because they are given only ten seconds or so over the instrumental ramp of music to talk, or told, "just read what we have written on the cue cards and no adlibbing. They were the great personalities, the great entertainers that really said something between the music; they entertained and attracted thousands of listeners to their sound."

Later, after the listener has left the control room shaking his head in dismay of what he has just experienced, the disc jockey reached over and pat's the microphone affectionately.

Speaking to it like it was the only friend he might have in the world—we might hear ...

"I could never make a living the way that listeners does. I can't image, to put five bolts on a car fender day in and day out. Amazing, what a waste of the mind, where is the creatively?"

A SPECIAL NOTICE About: "The DJ's Diaries!"

A WARNING

"If you've <u>ever</u> turned on a radio ... and called a DJ ... this book might be about ... YOU!"

Volume one is a collection of conversations and incidents that have taken place between disc jockeys and their listeners.

"It is **not** just stories recalling my years behind the microphone dealing with listeners (*you*) in front of the radio, but the recollections from '<u>hundreds</u>' of DJ's who recounted these stories from their own, **"DJ Diaries."**

Let me clear something up about DJ's.

We '*talk shop*' the same as you do about your work. We exchange stories about our everyday dealings with our listeners and sometime our fans—*YOU!*

From that came the years of condensing notes about those *'Remarkable'* conversations.

I think I can safely say that DJ's are no different than you when it comes to gossiping and those '*locker room stories*'! Reality is ... disc jockeys are *BETTER* at embellishing the facts! Thus confirming fact or fiction was not always possible due to the nature of some of the involvements. We have changed names, locations and radio station call letters to protect those we write about.

The Reasons will become obvious!

It must be noted—Most of the stories herein **do not represent most listeners, nor do all DJ's** experience what are contained on the pages of this book.

Statically, only about one percent of you that ever listen to a radio will *ever* call or *write* a DJ in your lifetime! An even smaller percent of these DJ's and listeners make up the stories that were gathered for this the first volume. (*See a special invitation to become a part of volume two later in this book.*)

"DJ Diaries; Radio's Remarkable Listeners" does clarify a few crazies--

Listeners do it with their ears!
Disk Jockeys do it with their mouths!
And without (YOU) the listeners!
There would be no (US) the disk jockeys!

CHAPTER 1

"And now ... here's the weather!"

Weather is the most talked about subject in the world. *(Good grief! It's hard to believe that sex is second!)*

Yes, my little listeners and radio buddies, weather is the perfect conversation starter between strangers, friends, lovers, enemies and so on. It's discussed, cussed, bitched about and used as the subject of good and bad jokes, but careful how you discuss weather if you include blaming that almighty power in the heavens.

Once I did a weather joke on the air about—

"Hey, eighty-two, and ... some rain today, oh poo on you-know-who for causing, uh no ... maybe I'd better be careful about that. Well, ha ha, I mean you know who might get struck by lighten"—-

BOOOOOOOOOOOOOOM!

True, I swear to-- *(Oooops, maybe no swearing).* Yes, out of nowhere this huge flash of lightning, followed by a large explosion rattled the control room. I nearly had a heart attack! The lights went out, and our transmitter's off-the-air warning bells and buzzers sounded the alarm all over the radio station.

The engineer, who always had a trusty flashlight strapped to his belt and our wide-eyed station manager, flew into the control room, both sure I had blown the transmitter to hell. Suddenly the lights and the transmitter popped back on the air before anyone could say anything.

I glanced over at the telephone and every phone line in the control room was blinking. Answering them as fast as I could, those who had heard my words of distain about *you-know-who* were all over me for my asinine antic. I got cursed, yelled at, and hung-up on by nearly listener that called.

Now, how about next time? No, no next time!

🎧 🎧 🎧

Ask any DJ and they'll tell you that weather forecasts are their **number one frustration.**

"Currently the temperature is seventy-four ... that's seven-four degrees at BXTZ radio," the DJ announces on the air.

About then the control room phone rings and once the DJ finishes the weather dialogue on the air he answers and hears ...

"Uh, hey bud," the caller says, "can you tell me what the temperature is right now?"

The DJ grits his teeth and grimaces. He strangles the telephone receiver and tells the caller in his best polite announcer voice, "its seventy-four degrees." Then he hangs up the phone and screams, "that's the fifth $#@&!* caller I've had to repeat the temp to in the last five minutes. Dear God is anyone listening to the radio today."

🎧 🎧 🎧

An even bigger problem with the weather pops up when listeners say the weather isn't going to do what the radio disc jockey says it's going to do.

2

One Arkansas listener had his own personal weather prognosticator ...

LISTENER; "You 'nouncers are wrong about that there weather report fur today. Yep, you see I got this here pet cricket and when he chirps like he's doin' now ... well you see, it is going to rain down raccoons and hound dogs. Yes sir-re.

(The cricket was right!)

THE TOP TEN LISTENER QUESTIONS ABOUT THE WEATHER

Disc Jockeys get asked a lot of strange things by listeners when it comes to the meteorological conditions. The votes are in and here is the best of the bunch as told to me.

- "Will it rain three months from now on July 16th?"
- "If it's partly cloudy sometime today will the rest of the day be partly sunny?"
- "Say you ever get a weather report saying anything about freezing dust?"
- "Can you tell me if those clouds over us today are empty?"
- Any chance that lightening might strike me while I'm sunbathing nude in the backyard?"
- "Hey, you ever heard of the wind blowing straight up and down?"
- "What size snowballs will it snow today?"
- Could you tell everyone we're going to have a blizzard? I really don't want to go to school today!"

- "I was just outside and I could see my breath. Do you know if it ever gets so cold that my words would freeze as I talked?"

🎧 🎧 🎧

A few winters back a popular DJ/Talk show host known for his controversial personality had this conversation *live on-the-air* with a lady caller.

DJ: " *...AND OHIO'S FORCAST FOR TONIGHT ... SNOW, ESPECIALLY INLAND EXPECT ABOUT SIX INCHES.*" *(Pause)* "*NOW, WE'RE BACK ON THE AIR TALKING TO YOU. HELLO, THIS IS LARRY O.*"

LADY CALLER: "*HELLO LARRY I WANT TO—*"

DJ: "*HELLO MY DEAR, SAY ... HOW MANY INCHES ARE YOU EXPECTING TONIGHT?*"

LADY CALLER: "*I ... I ...* (Click!!! BZZZZZZZZZZZZZ!)

🎧 🎧 🎧

Ever notice how sometimes the weather seems to stir up that feeling of, of—**"THE BEAST WITHIN!"**

Consider the senior citizen in Texas that didn't like the weather report he heard on the radio.

He got so mad he threw his radio out the window ...
The window was on the eighth floor ...
The radio (still playing) plummeted to the street ...
Bounced off the hood of a passing car ...
Scaring the poor lady driving the car so badly ...
She drove her car right thru a grocery
store's front window ...
Topping things off ...

The radio didn't break in the fall ...
And ... was still playing as the senior citizen was
arrested and hauled off to the police station!!!

🎧 🎧 🎧

Sometimes a listener can be too honest about the weather. This is the way the conversation went on the air in Indiana—

"It's still snowing this morning and the weather guy thinks there may be three or four feet of new flakes by tonight. Hello there JJ here, is it cold enough for you?"

"Oh, oh, gosh, I, I ... am ssssooooo, so c ... c ... cold. JJ, I ... I wanted to, uh to ... talk to you ... you about—"

"Wow, you do sound cold. What are you wearing at this very moment?"

"I ... I'm standing here in my ... my nightgown."

"You're nightgown? Oh gosh, if you're not warm enough on this snowy day it must be awfully thin?"

"Well," the lady listener giggled. "Uh, it is sort of—"

"You mean you can see thru it and all that, huh?"

"Uh, kinda, I guess. But JJ that's wha- not what I want to talk a ... a- about," the listener replied, still shivering."

"Wait! Listen, I got the best warm-up idea of the day. How about it," JJ the DJ questions, "are you game?"

"I don't know—?"

"Ah, come on it'll only take a minute, okay?"

"Okay," the lady listener responded uncertain.

"Here we go. First, take the telephone receiver and put it down the uh ... top, you know front of you know, between uh ... yes you know where."

"You mean like—"

Listeners can hear the muffled noise of the telephone receiver being stuffed down the front of the lady's gown.

"Like that?" The listener's voice can only be faintly heard because the telephone is nowhere near her mouth.

"FINE, JJ says. Then everyone on the radio hears ...

" A A A A A A A A A A G A A A A A A A A A A , HHHHHHHAAAAAAAAAAAA, GAAAAAAAAAAH, swish, pant, swish ... swish--!!!"

The DJ is breathing heavy, making sucking sounds, rolling his tongue around in his mouth, and shaking his head from side to side. In the background of the studio you can hear the voices of a couple of other people laughing and clapping on the air.

"Click! BUZZZZZZZZZZZZZZZZZZZZZZZZ!"

🎧 🎧 🎧

Ever heard this on a day when you think your sweat glands were steaming?

"Hot, hot, hot, hot, hot," the disc jockey announces on the radio in Arizona. "Man, its hot enough to fly eggs on a car hood."

Yep, a listener cracked a whole dozen eggs on the hood of his car.

It really worked! But when the listener tried to pry them off the hood the eggs had fried up so hard, he had to use a spatula to remove them.

By the way, the paint on the hood came off with the eggs.

The disc jockey eventually had to pay to have the listener's car hood, sanded and repainted!

🎧 🎧 🎧

Now---how about the story of the brilliant DJ who boasted that you'd more than likely freeze someone solid if a bucket of water was poured over his head?

Yes, in one nearly subzero winter a bunch of listeners did just that to a DJ. Not just once, but several times over the next couple of days. Plus, they poured water over the locks on his car's door handles. That froze up the locks. They even did the same thing to the doors on his apartment. Oh the poor, hapless DJ.

But in the end the DJ got the best revenge.

He showed up at a local bar in a bathing suit and got his picture in the newspaper the next day showing the patrons dumping a bucket of freezing cold water over his head. Oh sweet publicity.

My, what a disc jockey would or wouldn't do to get attention?

The bottom line; Understand this about what a DJ does to become well-known, to be the front and center attraction and be everything people are talking about.

> **"What's good for the radio stations ratings are good for the disc jockey."**

Sometimes it even means more $$$$$$$$$ too!

CHAPTER 2

" ...And What Would You Like To Hear?"

Y ou have a favorite song right? Right! It's that special song that you made memories to while listening to the radio. Then when you heard it on the radio later in life, those memories always flood back into your mind.

So when you want to hear your favorite song, you want to hear it over and over, again and again.

Now, if somehow you can't get enough of hearing your favorite song ... you call your favorite radio station and ask your favorite DJ to play it?

Ever wonder what that DJ goes through in an average night of taking listener request over the telephones when listeners call to request their favorite songs?

🎧   🎧   🎧

Try these **actual** listener/DJ conversations on for size during-
--**REQUEST TIME!**

"Radio TRXR, hi there, what you like to hear?"

"How about playing more fast songs?"

"Radio TRXR, hi there, what you like to hear?

"Hey dope! Why are all the songs you play fast songs? When you gonna play some slow songs, dummy!"

"Radio TRXR, hi there, what you like to hear?

"Hey boy, you got any Hank Williams?"

"Hank? Uh, no sir that's country music, we play only rock and roll music. Sorry I—"

"Hey," the caller cuts in. When the crap you long-haired hippies gonna grow up!"

"Radio TRXR, hi there, what can I play for you?

"Would you play the Beatles?"

"Uh, are you listening to us?" the DJ ask. "That's actually what I'm playing on the radio right now."

"I don't give a shit," the caller interjects, "play them again!"

"Radio TRXR, what would you like to hear?"

"I'd like to hear you shut your %$&# mouth!"*

"Radio TRXR, what song would you like tonight?"

"Is this radio station, TBRC?"

"No, this is radio station TRXR. You've dialed the wrong number, sorry."

"Well, give me their number. They play better music!"

"Radio TRXR, request line, what—"

"We want the Beatles! We want the Beatles!" It's the group that called earlier wanting the Beatles again.

It's pretty obvious the callers still aren't listening, because the Beatles song is still playing.

"Radio TRXR, hi there, what you like to hear?"

"What? Oh! I've been getting a busy signal for so long I forgot what song I was calling in to request ...!

"Request line, Radio TRXR, what's your request?"

"Is this uh, the request line?"

"Yes, Request line."

"Well, yes ... uh, let me see now, request ... uh"

"Your song request, what is it?" the DJ is getting a little put out.

"Oh, yeah, I uh ... is this TRXR radio, are you the DJ?"

"Yes, yes, wait ... hold on! My music's running out," I have to go on the air, the DJ tells the caller. "Hold on, stay on the line, okay?"

"Okay ..."

The DJ puts the listener on hold, and with his music fading, turns on the microphone and goes on the air doing what DJ's do, give the name of the Beatles song that has just ended, or maybe tell the time, and then punches the button to start three minutes of commercials. He picks the phone up and gets back to the listener. "Okay, man I'm sorry about that had to go, you know on the air and such ... Hello? Hello? Hello, are you there?"

The listener has hung up; the DJ shakes his head, and glances over at his eight incoming telephone lines. Every one of them is blinking with incoming request calls.

"Radio TRXR, what would you like to hear?"

"Hi man, I got this party going on right now, you see and I want you to play Elvis next and dedicate it to all my friends, here's their names. There's—"

"Sorry guy, I've got a long list of caller request that called before you. I'll get to it as fast as I can is ..."

"Hey M F ... play it now or your ass is grass!"

The DJ is used to this kind of thing; he gets several of those kinds of calls at night. It's hard to get listeners to realize there are more people listening to the radio any given minute that just one listener. He tried explaining that once and got hung up on.

In the mist of answering all the blinking request lines consider the disc jockey also has to think about the following;

- What he might want to say on-the-air when the song ends.
- Locate and line up the next song request he's going to play.
- Line up the recorded commercials he has got to put on the air when the song ends.

10

- Make sure all the controls and switches in front of him are in the right position to air those commercials he has got to run.
- Make sure the RIGHT REQUEST song is in the cue ready to air after the commercials end.
- Check the temperature reading.
- Again think about what he is going to say, quickly glance at the clock and ...
- ... turn on the microphone switch and somehow say, calmly, yet with bright and tight, smiling enthusiasm ...

"*TRXR rock and roll request, those were the Beach Boys, it's ten twenty-three and we're taking your request at three-three-five-four-four. Got one you'd like to hear? Give me a call. I'm taking yours right now. Outside now, raining. The TXTR weather guy calls for more tonight and currently in the super city its, seven five, seventy-five degrees. Hey, Radio TRXR wants you to know there will be a general meeting of the quilt and basket club tomorrow, downtown at one-five-eight Ellis Street. Meet time noon so ... bring your old army blankets ... ha ha, really now, kidding. They'll be working on a Gloria Vanderhoof designer blanket for the Taylor nursing home. Remember; don't miss this general meeting especially if you're a general.*"

Then he plays the commercials, and continues to answer the request lines. All this has happened in about ten minutes and he has nearly three hours and fifty minutes to go with the request show. He thinks about some of those hundred or so requests he'll rack up for song request this night. If each is say, four minutes long, will he get them all in?

Nope!

Will he still have listeners the next night?

Yep!

He takes one more call before he closes the request line for the night.

"TRXR radio, you got a request tonight?"

"Hello there, you sexy hunk of a man, I am turned on listening to you!"

"Uh ... hello, who is this?"

"Well ... you don't know me yet, but you did speak to me at that live broadcast you did last weekend at that car dealer," her voice is soft, smooth and sexy. *"You should remember me."*

"Mam, there were over a hundred people there and—"

"Hummmmm, I think you're cute," she coos. *"Say, when you get off work why don't you just come on over to my house and ..."*

"Uh, lady, this is a request show. I play request, so please, what would you like to hear."

"Well, I'd like to hear your heavy breathing as you shove it--!"

"Mam, Miss, or uh, Mrs." The DJ cuts her conversation off knowing where this is going. "I'm sorry, I'm sure my wife wouldn't approve of ..."

The woman hangs up on him. He's gotten these kinds of calls before and he'll get them again another night. Sadly, there are a lot of unhappy people out there. He even recalls a couple of lonely, 'you want to do it calls' from **MEN**!

Some disc jockeys will eventually give in and take that tumble with an unknown voice, but most will not! That is just what these memories are about from other *DJ DIARIES*.

🎧 🎧 🎧

As you've gathered by now when listeners call a radio station they don't always have a request for the DJ to play them a song. What follows are some more ...

REMARKABLE RADIO REQUEST!

- "Mister radio person ... would you please play the **Star Strangled Banner?**"
- "I'm a little pissed off at so and so. He's owed me a hundred dollars for over a year now, and I'd like you to go on the air and tell everyone that he doesn't pay his bills!"
- "Listen, I'm from the circus that's in town and we have lost this uh ... snake. We'd like you to tell your listeners to be on the lookout for it. Now, assure your audience that it's harmless, really. Shouldn't be hard to spot, its twenty feet long!"
- "Are you the fellow on the air? Good, I want you to get on the radio and tell my little girl to, **'come home this very minute!'** I know that she and her boyfriend are parked somewhere listening to the radio and this is the fifth time she's stayed out past midnight. Look, don't interrupt! I know that more than likely you can't say her last name, so just say, **'Cathy go home, your father is waiting up.'** What in hell you mean you can't do that on the air! #%$#&! Damn it, I'm on the city council and I know the owner of this radio station and I'll get you fired so fast ...!"
- "Could you tell everybody to go out in their yards and whistle for my dog? You see, she's old and on medications and I can't seem to find her."
- "Yes, I know all you play is rock and roll music but I'll give you five dollars if you'll play a song by **Doris Day** for me?"
- "I run this hamburger place down on sixth. One of your salesmen came by today and wanted me to buy some commercials, but I can't afford it. I tell you what I'll do

though. If you say, **'Harry's Hamburger's has got a two-for-one special ...** ' I'll give you five free burgers when you get off tonight. Nice deal, huh?"

- "Know what I'll do if you don't play that song you're playing right now ever again? I'll make you a cake!"
- I want you to tell everyone that at eight-thirty tonight, I'm having a beer bust at my house. I made a washtub of spaghetti and I'm new in town, and would really like to meet some people. Better yet, just invite some chick over, and come over yourself? What you mean you can't do that on the radio?"
- "Do you know that Jesus loves you? Get on the radio after this record and tell everyone that Jesus loves them too."

CHAPTER 3

"Keep Listening To Win!"

Radio stations run contest that give away money, cars, records, food, trips, concert tickets, raincoats, cattle, oil wells, a million dollars and more. In fact, anything that you can think of ... *as long as you keep your mind out of the gutter!*

Okay, how about the ... *KITCHEN SINK?*

Ah ha! Think you got me there, huh? Wrong!

Several years back the day came when my radio station ran out of prize ideas for their weekly—yes, weekly contest. *(We say that because seldom do you find radio stations that offer such things like that to keep listeners tuned in today.)*

Meantime, the sales manager remembered a client that owed the radio station money for commercials that had aired a few months in the past. The client was a plumbing and parts house. Voila! The account was closed as paid when the plumber gave the radio station a ... *kitchen sink!*

Not long after that, another radio station embellished on our idea. The kitchen sink they gave away was attached to a **Two hundred thousand dollar home!**

You might have guessed why radio stations give prizes away?

If you think your conclusion is because radio stations *love their listeners*, think again. The <u>BIGGEST</u> reason is it attracts MORE LISTENERS! MORE listeners a radio station can show that are listening equates into LARGER RATINGS and that my radio buddy is used to convince MORE ADVERTISERS to buy MORE commercials.

The end result ... **MORE MONEY FOR EVERYBODY!**

That aside, disc jockeys love to giveaway prizes, coupons for burgers, free drinks, movie passes, automobiles, even live animals and fish! True! It improves their ratings, which lets them keep their job for a few more months. It also brands them as hero's with some of their listeners—and in an odd sense, it makes some DJ's seem somewhat *'all powerful!'*

But things can backfire! It is the dark side of a DJ's nightmares.

First, the DJ has to deal with never knowing who is going to win and that listener's reaction to winning. Secondly, the DJ has to contend with all those people that call and are told they **lost!**

LISTENER ON PHONE WITH DJ: "Look, I can't ever seem to be the right numbered caller. If you ask for caller ten, I'm caller seven and so on, or the line is always busy. Next time, why don't you just hold me on the line till the next contest, then let me win it? Come on; tell me the answer to the contest. I'll split the cash prize with you. Hey, it'll be a secret between you and me. Okay?

LADY CALLER TO DJ: I tell you what honey. You let me win that grand prize and you know what I'll give you in return! *(Snicker ... O M G)!*

Of the entire seemingly insane contests that have happened over the years, radio people agree this one is the most tragic. All the classic warning signs and alarms were voiced, but the radio station ignored it all.

It happened in California. The radio contest was called ...

"HOLD YOUR WEE FOR A WII©"

The prize was a *Nintendo Wii©* video game system.

Those listeners were to drink as much water as possible without urinating to win.

As **'remarkable'** or better said, **absurd and stupid** as it sounded the contest went on the air.

Many potential contestants called, and there were eighteen finalists picked.

On the contest date, all were in the studio with the two DJ's that hosted the contest on the air. A lot of excitement was generated at the start of the contest and as it progressed the first of warning signs began to surface.

A listener started complaining after drinking nearly two gallons of water during the three hour limit. The DJ's simply laughed and made jokes about having to wiz.

Other warning signs began to surface when a few listeners called to say the contest was dangerous, even a nurse called and voiced that the contest could lead to death.

One listener was even quoted saying that drinking a huge amount of water could make people sick and they could even die from water intoxication.

One of the DJ's even asked the other, "Can that be true?"

The answer he got was, "Your body is 98 percent water, so not with water, why can't you take in as much water as you want?"

"Maybe we should have researched this before," commented the other DJ.

The contest ended and the lady that had complained of pains won second place and was awarded a pair of concert tickets.

The next day feeling ill, she called in sick. She then died in her bathroom only hours after the contest. Coroner's ruling was—

"Death due to water intoxication!"

The radio station was sued and went to court.

At the trail it was discovered that the contest details was to have been sent to the radio stations legal department, but wasn't!

The jury deliberated for two weeks and then returned a verdict delivering a total of $16.5 million dollars to the family of the woman.

Ten employees of the radio station were fired because of the contest.

A disc jockey in Kansas told the public he would be at a location he announced at a certain time covered with concert tickets. He announced, first come, first to win. He only had about 15 concert tickets still pasted to his body when he was arrested for, *'public nudity and disorderly conduct'*!

Here are some **REAL WINNNING** on-the-air-conversations!

PRIZE A: "Sir ... you have just won a lip-smacking pizza"
"Give it to somebody else, hoss'. I don't like pizza!"

PRIZE B: " ...and Miss So and So ... you have just won a trip to Mexico!"

"Oh darn, we just got back from there. Can't you give us something else? We'd really like to go to Japan!"

PRIZE C: "Yes sir, you've just won a six pack of **Coke**!"

"Ha, I'm sorry guy. I work for **Pepsi** better give me something else!"

PRIZE D: "Mam, your prize from radio Z-ONE today is an impressive, fully loaded, ready-to-go chain saw! Your husband is gonna enjoy this ..."

"I don't have a husband."

"Uh, well, it'll be a nice gift for your boyfriend."

"I threw that lazy #&@*$ (bleep!) ... out of the house last week!"

"Uh, mam ... Then maybe, maybe your Father would enjoy this chain saw."

"He's been dead for two years."

"Gee ... well uh ... you can always take it down to the hock shop and trade it in for a diamond ring, or some kind of girlie thing."

"Hey, first off don't call me a girlie, I'm a woman and secondly, I wouldn't be caught dead in a pawn shop!"

"Oh ..."

There are listeners that will do **ANYTHING** to win a radio contest. The bigger the prizes, the zanier the listener stunts will be.

They have jumped into vats of soupy, shaky jelly, dressed in diapers and covered their bodies with honey and feathers.

Some have built giant floats and painted huge signs with the radio stations call letters on them at their own expense. They have covered their new cars, even their bodies with radio station bumper stickers. They've danced non-stop for days and rode roller coasters for weeks at a time.

The *'Guinness Book of World Records'* credits one radio listener in Chicago with eating an eleven-foot tree to win a contest!

🎧 🎧 🎧

What would you do to win a contest?

Let your mind picture this; it's winter. The place is Wisconsin. The snow is a couple of feet deep and still snowing. It bitter cold. The wind chill temperature makes your teeth chatter and you can almost hear the wind howling through your brain. In the background, the music is fading and you hear—

DJ: *"Its seventeen degrees right now, but have no fear everyone ... I've go just the contest to warm things up. First, think of warm, sunny skies, cool ocean waters and the beach crowded with petty thing's laying all around you in their so firm, fully stacked and packed bikini's. Got the picture?"*

Listeners begin to hear beach and surfing music in the background backed with the sounds of seagulls and crashing waves.

DJ: *"Getting a little warmer, huh? Well ... I'm going to throw in the towel on that thought. Right ... a D A P T certified, think 'super summer' beach party towel ... but that's not all. To the first ten beauties that show up dressed in ... ha ha ... you got it, bikinis in the next hour each gets a towel AND we will draw the name of one of you tan tempting, beach bunnies to get an all-expense paid trip to the 'fun in the sun city—Miami, Florida." So get that bikini on now and snow surf it on down to the D A P T radio studios by one P.M."*

By one o'clock the studio and control room was packed with well over fifty ladies in bikinis. It was truly a 'DJ's bikini heaven!' The radio station photographer was having a field day along with most of the other radio staffers. The DJ had to draw names to pick the ten finalists. One was a five-year-old girl!

DJ: " ...Here's another finalist, honey for five years old you look smashing. See me kid, when you're about fifteen years older." The child's Mother beamed at the comments and getting her little child into the finals meant she just might win that trip to Miami.

DJ: " *...Now here's another finalist, who have we here?*"

The young woman seemed a little nervous. She bashfully whispered her name. She was still dressed in a heavy winter overcoat.

DJ: "*Now honey, I can't give you a radio D A P T 'think super summer' beach towel if you don't take off that heavy old overcoat. Come on now, don't be shy, the rest of you beautiful bikini babe's clap your hands, give the bashful babe some encouragement!*"

The studio and control room burst out with clapping and cheering then—

DJ: "*All right now ... yes sir, she's unbuttoning the coat. Guys' she's ... Now, off cccccccccooooooooooooooooooomes the ... the, coat and uh ... —Oh my!*"

The cheering and clapping suddenly stopped cold.

The lady was standing there in the control room ... **NUDE!**

The DJ relating the story said to this day he couldn't remember most of what he said on the air next or how he got out of the contest. Somehow, he stuttered through it, drew one of the other bikini ladies names to win the Miami trip.

"What in hell do you say to a naked lady standing right in front of you?" The D A P T disc jockey grinned. "I got through it by closing my eyes ... really and somehow keeping calm, pounced on the entry blank box and quickly drew a name and got into the winners spiel."

It was discovered that the lady was on her way to work when she heard about the contest on her car radio. It seemed a natural reaction for her to drive on out to the radio station thinking that no one in their right mind would show up there in such freezing weather to win a contest, especially as stupid as this one seem to be. Was she ever wrong!

She was a **TOPLESS DANCER** at a local club and was headed out to her job as she simply said, *" ...I was dressed for work!"*

🎧 🎧 🎧

A couple of DJ personalities doing a morning show often had girls to come into the station in bikinis to win stuff. The winners ended up surrounding the DJ's on a billboard advertisement for the radio station.

Then one morning the two offered a prize of a breast-enhancement procedure as a Christmas present from the radio station. Lots of talk good and bad, some including a group of ladies that picketed the radio station calling the contest, 'demeaning!'

"Hey, right or wrong, just get the call letters right in the breast-enhancement story for the rating books."

🎧 🎧 🎧

Believe it or don't!

I can truthfully say one time in Key West I saw one of those guys that seem to be mad at the world, protesting everything that walks or talks. In fact, he was at cussing at anyone and everyone that even looked at him.

Why? It would seem curious; no ... let's say the stupidest

thing I ever saw. He was not only was wearing the bondage studded collar, leather cloths, dirty torn T-shirt, a Mohawk haircut, and rings in every hole, lips, and any other place skin was exposed ... but no doubt the worst thing ever was he had tattooed on his forehead the word ...

"F--K"

So try and image this. A radio station DJ offered a six-figure payout if a listener would tattoo the radio stations call letters on their forehead.

One guy did it only to be told *'it was a joke!'*

I could never find out anything more about this, but hey, if you see the dork in Key West with the tattoo and if anyone is as stupid as him ... who knows?

🎧 🎧 🎧

Ever tried to win a radio station giveaway and **NEVER WON?** Frustrating isn't it?

You sit there dialing and dialing your little digits right down to the nubs only to hear the DJ on the radio say ... **"Hold your calls ... we have a winner!"**

There you sit mumbling under your breath with a few broken fingernails to show for your efforts and the urge to throw your coffee cup at something. We've heard stories of drivers trying to throw their cell phones out of closed windows. Scarier is the fact that they are dialing and driving at the same time!

A New Jersey DJ passed this story on to me ...

LADY CALLER: *"Say, my husband just went ape! What did you guys do to him? I mean he ... he was listening to the radio and he screamed at the top of his lungs, ripped the telephone right out of the wall. I'm calling you from a pay phone. Then, then ... he threw* *the telephone at the cat. Stranger still, he unplugged the radio, took it down to the basement, locked it in the food freezer and stormed out. He was gone about three hours and ... and when he came back he was ripped, you know ... roaring drunk. Right now, he's passed out in the kitchen. What in hell did you guys do on the radio station that made him so mad?"*

The lady was told that *maybe* it had something to do with the fact the radio station was giving away a set of **SUPER BOWL TICKETS!** It was suggested maybe her husband was calling, trying to be the one hundredth caller and he was caller ninety nine! *(Which was a pretty good guess, for it was true; he was the caller ninety-nine!)*

A week later the same lady called and wanted the radio station to buy her a new radio! (**They did!**)

🎧　🎧　🎧

Now comes a statement almost every disc jockey has heard more than once in their career—

*"**Listen you son-of-a-bitch! Your contests are all rigged! I know it; I'm going to report you to the FCC.**"*

The poor DJ, it seems the theory someone came up with a long time ago still holds true even today.

"THE LARGER THE PRIZE ...
THE MORE LOSERS WHO CALL TO TELL US WE CHEAT!"

Really! Seldom do these types of listeners seem to consider that a radio station ran the contest or promotion to draw first and foremost more listeners to get better ratings and etc ... Secondly, radio does want you to have *fun and maybe win something for nothing spent except for a little of your time!*

Remember, radio stations don't charge you to listen or to

play a contest. We don't even require you to call us if you don't want too.

Here's another listener class that DJ's hear a lot from—

"I know for a fact you $&#*#% don't really give away those #@%#& prizes! You just make up those @#$&$$ names that you say are winners, then you DJ #$@%$er's just block the &#$#%$ telephone lines so no one can call in. $#%& I'm right. You &%#$%$!!!!*

Try this next time you can't seem to win a contest, you can't get through for the busy signals because about anywhere from fifty to a hundred or more callers are calling the same time you are ... wait a few minutes after the contest is over then call. When the DJ answers thank him or her for doing something *nice* that was *fun* and *free* that you could get involved in.

It'll leave the DJ **speechless!**

Okay, has there ever been radio contest or deceptive promotions that radio stations and/or disc jockeys have cheated on you ask?

Maybe, but we're sure it would be an infinitesimal amount. Fact is, so far no one has ever come to me with a story of a station fixing a contest. Could be this book will generate a story about cheating radio stations or DJ.

If it happened, we'd tend to think they were caught, fired and fined. You can bet your bottom dollar that today, most hard working radio pros would *never—ever* try it. The stakes are too high.

Rules and regulations on how a broadcast facility operates are defined quite clearly by the *Federal Communications Commission.* (FCC)

Those rules can be grounds for a DJ to lose his job, be fined more money than most make in two years or more, and ... he might even land in jail!

There is also a larger threat of losing the opportunity to even work in radio again. For instance; would you cheat in a contest if a ten thousand dollar fine and a jail sentence was a real possibility? Would you do it if the radio station where you worked also lost its license to broadcast? A license which in some cases, could be worth *millions of dollars*!!!

🎧 🎧 🎧

RADIO MOVES THE MASSES!

As humans, we are the only species that turns on that magical box for companionship and more.

Oh dear, I nearly forgot to make exceptions for that sweet little lady listener with the parakeet who only chirps when the radio is turned on. Or the listener that called to say his chickens won't lay eggs unless they are listening to—*(But those listener stories are somewhere else in these remarkable stories!)*

In turning on the radio we react to what we hear is so many ways. In the early days of radio, listener's ears would be exposed to about every kind of radio show you could image. Including radio pitch men selling all sorts of quackery from medicines that would cure nearly every disease known to mankind to electric girdles that would not only slim down ladies bodies but increase the libido!

Then in 1923 along came the, *"Goat Gland Doctor!!*

John R. Brinkley, who after only three years of medical school and a 'diploma mill' doctor's degree opened a radio station in Wichita, Kansas to spread his message that claimed ...,

"Sexual glands from the male goat would restore the 'virility' of

older men!' After all, the image of love down through the ages had been depicted as the mythical creature, Pan. Half man, *half goat!*

"Dear gentlemen friends out there in radio land, do you feel like a eunuch? Has your lust for life left you listless? Listen to this amazing, love life saving cure!"

His claims would make him over a million dollars a year and in the 1920's during the Great Depression that was a fortune.

Eventually, the good doctor claims were scrutinized by the Federal Government that issued radio station license to broadcast. He moved from Kansas down to Del Rio, Mexico and built one of the first *'Boarder Blasters,'* radio stations with more power than any commercial radio station in the United States. There he would continue to pitch his story over the radio waves that reached most of American and many foreign countries.

I first heard that story when I worked at the very radio station that first broadcast his miracle claims, KFDI in Wichita, Kansas. Maybe because of Dr. Brinkley, or maybe not, the radio station which at one time had been known as KFBI changed its call letters a couple of times. You won't find a radio station today with 'FBI' in their call letters.

Curious about Brinkley, I even bought and recommend the book, *"The Bizarre Careers of John R. Brinkley"* authored by R. Alton Lee and published by the University Press of Kentucky, Lexington, Kentucky.

Another side note; this same radio station was also once owned by *'America's Sweetheart,'* Mary Pickford!

That was one of the first incidents that perked up the ears of the government. Slowly, more and more **FEDERAL** laws to control technical operations and content of radio stations broadcast were enacted because of the likes of Brinkley and another famous radio broadcast created over seventy years ago.

Sunday, October 30th, 1938

On that day, at age 23 before he became a famous Academy Award Actor, Orson Welles, was a young broadcaster, theatrical playwright, radio director and producer. Inspired by the works of H. G. Wells 1898 novel, "War of the Worlds" Orson would convince thousands of people that Martians had invaded the Earth. Many would run into the streets in panic, police departments were dispatched to protect areas of the New Jersey and New York areas. The havoc created that night made him and his Mercury Theater Players famous for the 'fake' broadcast.

In doing so, in that one hour Orson pulled off one of the greatest hoaxes in history of Broadcasting.

Oddly enough, before the show even started it was announced that the evenings performance would be in honor of '*Halloween*,' featuring that talented staff of actors preforming on, "The Mercury Theatre on the Air."

If you've ever heard the old radio show, or seen one of the countless movies or articles of history about "War of the Worlds," you will come to understand the 'mind-set' of that generation of radio listeners in the thirties. Please look it up on your computers, visit your library, or ask an old disc jockey that has more than likely has heard the show more times that he can remember.

Today I still take *Jeff Wayne's 1978 musical concept album of "War Of The Worlds,"* on my *Kindle Fire* when I travel.

🎧 🎧 🎧

"There a sucker born every minute!" a phrase that some say is credited but not true, to P. T. Barnum, showman, business man, and credited to be the best known sham artist and instigator of hoaxes of all time.

Image, your phone rings and the voice on the other end tells you that you have won, **"GREAT PRIZES!"**

There are some sick, twisted minds out there in radio land.

It is the person that *pretends* to be a disc jockey and calls an *unsuspecting* person and tells them they have won all kinds of fantastic prizes.

Later, when those poor people come by the radio station to pick up their prize it is sad having to tell them that the radio station wasn't running a contest or giving anything away.

Like the DJ that told us about the senior citizen in a wheel chair who struggled into a cab, and arriving at the radio station pulled herself up a ramp and through the door into the studio to be told she had been the butt of a cruel telephone caller.

Or the disc jockey and nearly the whole radio staff trying to explain to a very irritated man that had just driven *fifty miles* into town to pick up his new car that, *'there was no car!'*

Today, most contests that are on the air have the listener call the radio station *first* to win something rather than the radio DJ calling them.

But alas, nothing is perfect. Try and explaining to a very irate Mother that her baby girl who can be heard crying in the background *didn't win tickets* to see a famous teen singing idol that was coming to town because ... there were no tickets—

You get the picture.

We recommend if someone calls you and tells you that you have won something from a radio station ... call the radio station and verify it immediately!

CHAPTER 4

"The Good Guys!!!"

D epends on how you look at it. *'Good Guy'* was a term used by some radio stations in the late 60's to describe those, *'Magnificent Men of the Microphone!'* It was an image of nonchalant, clean-cut, crew-cut young men wearing headphones, white buck shoes and blazers jackets in the stations colors. Carrying slim, pencil-thin shiny microphones, smiling and ready to leap on a stage, any stage there was a live audience. They defined an audience as, *'Anywhere there were more than two people standing still in one place!'*

Exposed as they were and still are to the public via the 'airwaves' and personal appearances, disc jockeys can sometimes lose that 'good guy' image. They commit the sin of ignoring the deadliest radio rule;

NEVER BECOME PERSONALLY INVOLVED WITH A LISTENER!

It's the quickest way a DJ can get a reputation—the wrong kind, and it usually spreads faster than a news bulletin. Breaking that rule has caused many a DJ to be fired—even black balled in the media business.

It has cost some their very *LIFE!*

Most of the time the DJ is tempted to become entangled with a listener for the same reason that listener becomes involved with a DJ.

That age old curiosity to see what that voice looks like in person.

🎧 🎧 🎧

Good Guy DJ Cliffie Z loved women.

Pretty, homely, plump, thin, tall or short had little or nothing to do with it. Nightly, he answered his request lines like a man possessed!

It was like big game sports fishing. "Play the bait, watch 'em strike and reel 'em in," he would say.

At the end of his air shift, he'd head home *in a different direction every night!* Where ever he was invited is where he would show up.

It was always easy keeping up with 'Good Guy' Cliffie Z's status.

When he didn't get a *'strike'*—you'd find his car in the radio station's parking lot loaded down with his clothes and Cliffie snoring soundly on the couch in the lobby. He'd always be up and out of the radio station before the day staff and the boss arrived. Sometimes when he didn't get a chance to shower for one reason or another his day would be filled trying to find a place to bathe and clean up.

When he did *'reel one in'*—he'd telephone the radio station for a wake-up call for the next morning.

It would always be a different phone number!

Eventually, the odds caught up with Cliffie. He really got bugged about the *'little bug'* the doctor told him he had picked up. That was only the start of his troubles. Getting one young lady pregnant didn't set too well with the girl's father who was the *'CHIEF OF POLICE!'*

Last we heard Cliffie Z is still one great DJ today—at one of your better known STATE PEN'S! Some of the tougher inmates will even tell you he's still a pretty good *'GOOD GUY!'* Oh my!

🎧 🎧 🎧

The most *'REMARKABLE LISTENER/DJ'* entanglement story ever told to me was when I sat down and over dinner in the Florida Keys with Stan 'the rock'n radio man.'

"I was working in the majors, you know the big time and I didn't get there by getting into listeners panties. No way, ever man!!" Stan started. "I was a married to a beautiful woman and we had three kids I adored. It had taken me six years of mental murder to land this gig."

He went on to say his first six months were pretty normal. The request lines rang off the hooks and his personal appearances were fairly well attended by a growing base of listeners. Then one day, a lady called that caught Stan's attention.

"In broken English, she told me that she and her sister had just moved to America a few months back. She had met and married an important scientist that had visited her native country ... Italy. He was rich and had brought both sisters back to the states. She went on to tell me that they listened every day and liked my show. She wondered if her younger sister, who was too bashful to ask could come down and see what a radio station looked like."

It wasn't an unusual request and Stan extended the invitation for the ladies younger sister to come down. A couple of day later the young, pretty sister showed up. Stan showed her around and they had coffee. It was then she told him that her older sister was unhappy with her marriage. Her sister, she said, was married to a very rich old man who was seldom home.

"I didn't give it much thought at the time. Coffee talk crap, you know. The kind of stories we've all heard before," Stan recalled. "A couple of days later, I'd forgotten about the visit and the sisters."

Then Stan got another call from the older sister. It was to thank him for being so nice to her little sister and she extended an invitation to join her and her husband as guests at one of the most expensive restaurants in the city.

"I tried to tactfully decline, but she insisted that since I had been such a gentleman to her baby sister that her husband, Dr. X would be honored." Stan smiled, and continued. "Dr. X was one of the greatest minds in the world today. I guess I got caught with my mouth opened, because before I could close it I'd pretty much been roped into the invitation. Still, I tried to get out of it, telling her I'd have to alert my wife and get a baby sitter for the kids. But before I knew it, she'd told me it was too late to do all that. She'd already sent her limo to pick me up."

Stan continued to backpedal, telling her that he wasn't dressed for the occasion but she told him not to worry—her husband owned the restaurant. It was just one of his many holdings. Trapped, Stan called his wife and simply told her he was going to get home late.

"After all, it all pretty much seemed plausible; I mean her husband was going along with all this stuff, right?"

When Stan finished his show and went out front of the radio station ...

"What a surprise, there it was a real honest-to-God limo waiting for me. Like something out of the movies. A block long, a bar and color TV in the back and a chauffeur dressed in black who spoke only Italian." Stan rubbed his beard, and then laughed. "VIP, all the way baby, first class. The chauffeur handed me a note and then we proceeded to cross town to the dinner date."

The note said that the professor and his wife were already at the restaurant and expecting Stan. A larger surprise awaited Stan when he stepped off the elevator thirty-five floors above the city into the classy bistro.

"When I told the head waiter who I was," Stan started, "he clicked his heels, pressed a gold key in my hand and escorted me back into the elevator with instructions to use the key in the switch near the up buttons.

"Hell, the buttons didn't even show a thirty-sixth floor and I had that first inkling of that old, 'warning bell' tinkling in my head."

The elevator door opened again and Stan found himself in a penthouse suite. The floor was marble, with what looked to be a gold inlay pattern. Just past the modern contemporized living room on a raised level was an immaculate dinning room. Chrome lined floor to ceiling windows, reflected a huge table with ornate settings for four. Outside, those windows the entire city skyline blinked back at him.

Sitting at the table was the younger sister that had visited Stan at the radio station. She was dressed to kill in a tight, low-cut, sea-blue sequined evening dress.

"Oh man, did I really start to feel underdressed." Stan whistled. "She was stunning, gorgeous, like something out of an Italian movie. She told me that the Dr. and her sister would be along shortly." Stan felt a bit more relaxed. "But still, way off in the distance it seemed that warning bell in my mind was ringing a little louder."

Small talk ensued, a few cocktails served by a maid helped past the time while the two waited for the rest of the party to arrive. Stan talked about his radio life and she talked about how lucky she and her sister were to be in America.

Had he ever been to Italy? Did he speak her language? Then, about thirty minutes into their conversation the phone rang. A butler brought the phone to the sister and after a short conversation in Italian; she hung up and looked dejectedly at Stan. It seemed that her sister and husband had forgotten another dinner engagement they'd scheduled to attend.

"But—"she brightened, and told me they had promised to try and get by later for drinks. "Now at that moment I swear something screamed at me in my mind to say goodbye but ..." Stan paused, " ...what the hell, I didn't want to seem like a clod. I mean, she'd gone to a lot of trouble on account of me. You know; the limo, the dinner and all so ... I stayed and ate."

After the meal the maid came back out of the kitchen and said something to the young woman in Italian. Getting up she excused herself to go to the kitchen saying she had some instructions to give the kitchen help.

Meantime, Stan noticed that the butler was in the living room turning down the lights and putting soft romantic Italian music on the stereo.

"Image this now," Stan resumed, "I'm standing there now imagining hearing more bells chiming in my mind. Telling me something wasn't kosher in 'richer-than-shit' land. Then a noise over by the elevator brought me back to my senses. Out of the corner of my eye I caught a glimpse of the butler, maid and the rest of the kitchen help in the elevator as the doors slide closed."

Stan bolted over to the elevator. Now it really was time to leave! Sticking the elevator key into the slot he discovered to his amazement—it didn't work! Later, he would find out it took a different key to activate the elevator from the penthouse level.

It was at that time a soft, sexy voice behind him caused Stan to spin around.

"Yeah, right ... you think you can guess the rest of the story, huh?" Stan sputtered, speaking through a mouthful of food. "You'd be right and wrong at the same time, buddy."

"Standing in front of me was the younger sister dressed in

à thin, see-through, no-holds-barred, negligee. It blew me away, man. My alarm system overloaded, this was one fine shapely female. She had more curves than a mountain road and yep, we did the whole wild and wicked sex trip!"

"But with all the rights and wrongs of what happened there's a twist," Stan laughed. "The tale ain't been totally told ... yet."

As they lay in bed afterwards gazing out over that jeweled skyline she told Stan the whole truth and nothing but the whole truth.

Stan paused to take a large gulp of his dinner drink then continued.

SHE HAD NO SISTER!!!

"I jumped up like someone has just shoved a microphone up my ass! I must have looked pretty stupid standing there in her round bed, stark nude."

Not only did she confirm that she didn't have a sister, but she told Stan that it was one of her maids she had make the call pretending to be the older sister so he wouldn't suspect her voice.

"Yes, she wanted to see the face connected to the ... as she put it ... that *handsome voice*. You know how that goes, right?"

(We pause for Station Identification)

Yes, like I said, every disc jockey I've ever spoken with always had someone that wanted to know what they looked like. In fact, years ago I had a woman with the sexiest voice I ever heard record a series of comedy bits to use on DJ radio shows called, *'SILLY SEXY SHOW-STOPPERS!'* I sold a few sets of the recording to other disc jockeys and got a lot of laughs from those that called me to say I sure was lucky to work with such a sure-fire sultry, sexy woman! I don't think even they pictured the fact that this woman weighed nearly three hundred pounds!

Now, back to Stan the Rock'n Man.

"She told me that she really did have a husband and he really was the rich and famous Dr. X but—he was old and didn't enjoy sex. Now, here's the shocker ..." Stan paused and watched me for a reaction. " ...she told me he even knew about me! He approved with this, uh, seduction— *If it made her happy.*"

"Hell, Dave ... I had never cheated on my wife and you know as a jock yourself how often we get the chance with all those lonely callers, but ... no way! Stan swore, "to this day I can't image how I got sucked into this one time. It was all so above the norm you know?"

Later, driving home Stan told himself that no matter how crazy, weird—but yet, pleasant the whole sensuous scenario had been he would never, never again get involved with this woman!

It was a promise Stan could not keep.

Two or three days later, as he was going through his fan letters he noticed one letter in particular. It had no return address.

"When I opened it, I about crapped my pants!"

Five, one-hundred dollar bills fell out and floated to the floor. Stan ripped the envelope to shreds looking for a note. There was none.

"I stared down at that green stuff on the floor," said Stan. "Who had sent this and why? This was freaky, but I knew immediately this was money I couldn't keep. Could it be payola from a record promoter, an advertising client?" He also remembered the radio station payola agreement he'd signed a while back, DJ's taking money was against the law, a Federal law! Was this a test of loyalty to the radio station?

He picked up the money and stuffed it in his pocket and went on the air.

Later, Stan was crusin' along their air waves, being his wild and crazy self, playing songs, cracking jokes and taking request when—

"There she was on the phone! It should have dawned on me, she'd sent the money. That was the last straw. I asked her for her address, for ... by God, I was going to send the money back!"

This started the woman crying. She then told Stan that the money had not come for her, but from her husband!

"Image that," Stan spoke, taking a sip of dinner wine. "That old fart had sent it. Again, I demanded to know her address, but she refused. I was really pissed off at this point and slammed down the telephone receiver. At about the same time, my record had faded and a long stretch of silence told me my show was gonna go downhill the rest of the day!"

Getting off the air the still irritated Stan called information only to find out that Dr. X's telephone number was unlisted.

"So, I socked the money away in my desk. I sure as hell didn't want to get home and have my wife discover the bread!"

Stan didn't sleep very well that night and the next day at work he asked the news director if he knew of an address for the famous Dr. X.

"News directors have their sources, and when I got the address from him ... I by damn drove out to their house. It was in the ritziest section of the suburbs. There was a guard on the gate. I tried talking him into calling the house or letting me in but ... he refused my demands."

Another day passed and Stan got too busy with work to deal with the problem of the five hundred bucks.

Then, on a Friday his boss informed him at the last moment, as usual, that Stan would have to make a personal appearance at a local night club.

"The money up-front ... two hundred and twenty-five bucks," Stan recalled. "Those kinds of things are sometimes a pain in the ass, but good bucks. I figured, what the hell, I could filter a couple of hundred of that five-hundred into the pot to appease my wife."

It usually isn't the rule of things but some radio wives are a slightly jealous of their husbands' star treatment, even as weak as it is today, Still, every dollar helps the homestead, so they try and understand.

"We tell 'em a job is a job," Stan defends radio. "You're a pro. So you go, appear, smile, tell some corny jokes from the bandstand, slap the owner of the bar on the back and tell him what a great place he's got. Then you mingle some with his customers, shake a few hands, except a few free drinks, maybe pat a few ladies on the rear and let one or two of them pinch yours. Then you get the hell out of there and head for home. It's really routine, normal stuff ... right?"

By now the way this story was going, I knew Stan wasn't in for anything normal.

"I arrived at the address and at first, figured I was at the wrong place because the outside neon lights were off, but a sign on the door said this was the right club. So, figuring I was early I pounded on the door."

The guy that opened it was huge.

"I mean hunk, l-a-r-g-e," Stan spelled out, "as in ape."

As he had guessed, he was early. The band was setting up and this heavyweight sun blocker that had opened the door then went over behind the bar, opened up the till, counted out two-hundred and twenty-five dollars and handed it to Stan, and poured him a free drink.

"Getting the lay of the club and figuring I needed some more into, I got up and was crossing the danced floor heading in the direction of the band when a door opened near the bandstand."

It was her!

"What an incredible shocker, huh, can you believe it? I've never be speechless, hey ... we're disc jockeys! I had to deal with this, end this now." Stan scraped a piece of lobster around his plate, and then put the fork down. "She told me that you-know-who had bought this place for her as a wedding present, since she loved to dance so much, and it was also a good investment for him."

She'd had Stan booked for the appearance and made arrangements at the same time for the club to be closed.

"Scary ... what you can do with money!"

To make matters worse the lady had bought Stan a surprise present. Stan looked at me across the table with a sour expression. Leaning on both elbows, he resumed this remarkable tale.

"My hands were shaking. I don't know if it was from being hacked—off at being set up again, being used again or a little fearful of Mr. Muscles behind the bar who was watching us like a hawk."

Reluctantly, Stan opened the package, inside a *Rolex* watch.

"You know what those things cost! It was crazy, what you think about when you've lost control of a situation." Stand shook his head, "Nothing in my mind wouldn't equate with anything sensible, I was numb."

The band kicked off with a good old rock and roll song and the lady dragged Stan onto the dance floor and the night was underway. Later, they got it on in the back office on the thickest, deepest shag carpet Stan shore he'd ever seen.

"As I drove home with the watch hidden under the car seat, I just couldn't image the money it must have cost to keep the club closed on a busy bar night," Stan said then laughed. "To pay a band, a bar tender, body guard, bouncer or whatever ... I'd been had ... again, paid for a personal appearance which really was, should I say performance!"

The next day the lady called Stan while he was on the air. He tried to reason with her. "I told her there were hundreds, thousands of guys she could pick and choose from, but nooooo ... she liked me.

He started seeing her on a pretty regular basis. "Get this," Stan frowned, "we even started using a motel that her husband owned closer to the radio station for uh, early lunch. Yeah, right, I'm sure you believe that."

They met in the penthouse several more times and like clockwork, she kept sending him five hundred dollars a week. He wasn't happy about the money, but nothing he said could convince her to stop sending it.

"She'd just laugh and blink those big doe eyes and say ... 'oh-hon-nee, you-a good guy, you-a deserve-uh dee's tings!'" Stan mimicked. The amount climbed to around five thousand dollars. Finally, he took some of it home telling his wife it was a 'bonus' for good ratings.

Stan started not to care. He lied to his wife abut weekend business trips.

"More than once pal," Stan said, slowly. "We spent a weekend on Dr. X's yacht. Flew to Vegas a couple of times, hell we even did it at their thirty room mansion when the good doctor was out of town."

Stan was burning the proverbial *'candle at both ends'.* It was like an addiction, the money, the glamor, the places, not to mention a knockout gorgeous, *sugar Mama* so to speak. He was floating above all reproach until—

"My running around all hours, telling the wife one thing, and trying to assure the boss that all was well at home was catching up with me. My work started to suffer; I got a couple of warning from the boss. Then without warning, the shit hit the fan."

Stan was served with divorce papers. His wife was throwing the book at him.

"She ... she nailed me with a stupid blunder on my part," Stan started, his eyes misting over. "She was friends with the boss's wife and one day she innocently called and told her to thank her husband for the nice bonus ... and well, the rest is history. My wife hired a detective, who had pictures and such; I didn't have a leg to stand on."

End of the story?

"Not quite," Stan grimaced as if someone was twisting his arm. "I lost my job over the divorce mess, bad image for the radio station you know. I didn't detest because of the pictures the wife had that I figured would end up in court or maybe even the newspaper. But later, it finally struck me as odd that the pictures didn't surface during the divorce trial."

I realized where his story was headed. Dr. X paid Stan's wife off not to use the pictures!

"Had to be that, just had to be!" Stan shook his head. "Very hard to believe that, but my ex only laughed at me when I approached her with the question."

What about Dr. X's wife?

"This whole mess wouldn't just disappear. Oh, she was sympathetic and some comfort. Really, she was sort of there because I needed ... needed, something, uh ... somebody. I don't know man; she was still sex hungry for me. Why I didn't know. She even convinced her husband to let me move into a room at the motel he owned till I could pull myself together."

The one day Stan was sitting on the motel room's bed, a little woozy and tipsy from downing a six pack of beer, feeling a bit blubbery and sorry about everything. The doorbell rang and thinking it was the motel maid Stan yelled out that the door was unlocked.

It was Dr. X!

"I'd never met or talked to him, but I'd seen pictures of him on the TV news and magazines. At that very moment, I wanted to jump off the bed and stomp his face. Somehow, this well-groomed, wrinkled old bastard had been behind all my disasters."

Second guessing Stan's thoughts Dr. X reached back quickly and opened the motel room door. Standing outside, blotting out the sunlight was the chauffeur and the trained monkey from the night club. Stan dropped back down on the bed like a ton of crap.

"Dr. X closed the door, smiled and then told me the way it was to be."

First, his wife was pregnant!

Stan felt his heart skip a beat.

"Secondly, the Doctor went on to tell me that he was happy for that fact."

Then according to Stan, Dr. X smiled, and tossed something at him.

"Scared the crap out of me at first," Stan explained. "I was surprised to see that it was a cigar."

"Thirdly," Stan went on, "the Doctor raised a crooked, shaking finger and gestured it at his own crotch. Then, with much emphasis, he told me that his wife's child was his. Get that? That the kid was his!"

At that moment it all hit home. Stan realized that he had been totally manipulated from the beginning!

"Good God ... do you believe it, I'd been paid and played to be the breeder bull, nothing more!"

For a full minute Stan and Dr. X glared at each other.

"Finally, Dr. X waved his arm, pointed at me again, and told me we were about to reach a little agreement."

The doctor reached into his coat pocket. Stan shut his eyes and wondered if a dead person heard the gun that shot him.

He heard the doctor calling him a fool and telling him to open his eyes. "He was handing me an envelope and I wanta tell you exactly what he told me."

Stan's expression changed, it took on an 'older look' as his voice became raspy, and he started to talk again.

"My boy, when I leave—you will open that envelope,

understand? It has my personal attorney's address and phone number. You will call him for instructions and Stan, after that time you will never, never, try to contact him, me, my wife, or my child after it is born or ..." he waved a hand over his shoulders, " ...a few of my more capable employees will find you, and it will become rather messy. Is that clear? You may speak now."

Stan told of blurting out the word, yes and was about to say something else when Dr. X interrupted him.

"Stan, listen to me closely, you know I have got the power to do things you could never dream of, and you have experienced some of it you know. Those men outside this door are my wife's brothers. They are ... how should I say it, Stan, bad, real bad men. Never come to this city again; never mention our name, ever and you will be okay."

Dr. X opened the motel room door and walked out.

"But he never walked out of my life," Stan said to me as he motioned for the waitress. "After the doctor left I opened the envelope and in it was ten thousand dollars cash!"

The call to Dr. X's lawyer got him a briefcase with half a million dollars with the assurances that he'd get another five thousand dollars a month as expenses.

"I can't complain," Stan says getting up, "I managed to patch things up enough to at least send some of that money to get both of my girls weddings paid for and my boy in college. Although I was ready to kill him once when he told me that he wanted to quit college and be a DJ like his old man had been. But ..." Stan grinned, "He snapped out of it when I threatened to cut off the monthly allowance I was sending him."

Leaving the restaurant Stan had only one other thing to say about this most remarkable story.

"I got lucky, retired on some wise investments, but you know what? If I had it to do all over again, I'd never have played around with a radio listener. Never, ever man, no way!"

CHAPTER 5

"How About A Word From Our Sponsor?"

L et's hear it for the commercials!
Come on now gang; would everyone that *loves* commercials stand up? Uh … if you *LIKE* commercials how about standing up?

Okay, does anyone have to go to the bathroom?

Hey, commercials are the *'bread and butter'* of broadcasting. Yes, we know you're bombarded with a billion dollars' worth of them a year, still …

… ask any radio listener, and you'll find his or her tolerance for commercials are a few points in popularity below a *'trip to the dentist'*. But you know what? Without them radio couldn't come to you by the flick of a switch for *FREE!*

Sure, if disc jockeys had their choice about commercials they wouldn't play them either—but consider what you'd hear on the radio instead.

<u>DISC JOCKEY:</u> "IT'S TEN-OH-SIX IN THE BIG CITY … AND HERE'S ANOTHER BIG HIT AND THAT'S THE WAY ITS GONNA BE IF … YOU CONTINUE TO SUPPORT COMMERCIAL FREE RADIO.

LISTEN PEOPLE, MY WIFE AND CHILDREN HAVE GOTTA EAT … IT'S BEEN TWO WEEKS OF BEANS AND MORE BEANS. BABY, NEEDS NEW BOOTIES AND MY MOTHER-IN-LAW HAS

BEEN DIPPING INTO OUR COOKIE JAR TO GET ENOUGH MOO-LA TO PLAY THE HORSES.

PLEASE, PRETTY PLEASE DON'T FORGET EVERY OTHER PENNY YOU CAN SEND THE RADIO STATION WILL GO TO HELP PURCHASE SOME NEW MUSIC. I MEAN MAN; SOME OF THIS MUSIC IS LIKE ... SO OUT OF STYLE.

SO EVERYONE, EVERYWHERE ... KEEP US ON THE AIR, SEND YOUR MONEY, YOUR DONATIONS TO ... KEEP RADIO FREE OF COMMERCIALS, OUR ADDRESS IS—"

Get the picture? It's still a commercial because without them, there would be no music, no news, no sports, no information, no contest OR disc jockeys on the radio. Fact is radio as you know it wouldn't exist.

Commercials are the least understood part of radio. In fact, do you know how rich your favorite DJ would be if he or she had a nickel for every time someone called up and asked ...

"Why do you have to play all those commercials?"

Oh, almost forgot. You need to add the following to the above question. %#%&*@ and a few ... #@%$& so the DJ will understand that you are truly *%#$&#!-off about all those #$@#& commercials!

🎧 🎧 🎧

In the busy world of the DJ's, we don't have the luxury to ignore commercials. Remember, we are trying to keep the action moving forward. We are stuck in that little studio with the commercials. But note; we seldom hear a whole commercial. But we sure know how one starts and how one ends. It is those 'key words or cue' points, or tags we must be aware of to move to the next thing on our agenda, music, news or whatever.

So, here is what happens when some DJ's are at their wits end having to listen over and over and over ... YEEEEEEE!

COMMERCIAL: "REMEMBER, WHEN YOU ARE BOTHERTED BY THE PROBLEM OF HEMORRHOIDS ... GET *PREPARATION H!*"

The next song the DJ played ... ***"Ring of Fire!"*** by Johnny Cash

COMMERCIAL: "COME ALIVE ... YOU'RE IN THE *PEPSI* GENERATION!"

DJ Says ... "Right you are—drink Pepsi and come alive all over your neighbor's lawn!"

COMMERCIAL: "YES, SO AND SO SAYS, WE AREN'T MONKEYING AROUND ... THIS BRAND NEW 19_ _ BUICK CAN BE YOURS FOR ONLY THREE THOUSAND AND FORTY-FOUR BANANAS!"

A day or so later a clever listener showed up in the Buick dealer's showroom with ... THREE THOUSAND AND FORTY-FOUR BANANAS!

At first the dealer thought it was all a big joke—but not the listener, he brought along his lawyer.

Listener and lawyer drove away in a brand new Buick!

If that wasn't enough, they drove out to the radio station that had run the commercial and left the DJ who had done the commercial a tip of ONE HUNDRED BANANAS!

🎧 🎧 🎧

Is it really true that the most fantastic, one-of-a-kind, once-in-a—lifetime bargain you have ever purchased is that *BRICK BAT* you use as a door-stop?

In a recent survey conducted by this author, the following statements were gathered from four out of five DJ's who responded to the question ...

"DO YOU EVER GET LISTENER CALLS THAT ARE CRITICAL ABOUT THE COMMERCIALS YOU PLAY ON THE AIR?"

Below are parts of commercials and what some listeners called up to tell the disc jockey about them—

"...MORE DOCTTORS RECOMMEND ..." "My doctor never heard of it!"

"...TASTES AS GOOD AS ..." "According to who? Who #$%$ cares!"

"...FOR INSTANT RELIEF ..." "Hey, &$#% it still aches!"

"...LARGE AND SENSUOUS ..." "A bath towel never turned me on!"

"...THE QUICK PICKER UPPER ..." "Never picked me up anywhere!"

"...CLEANS AND CONTROLS ..." "The sink today, world tomorrow!"

"...STRONG ENOUGH FOR A MAN, BUT MADE FOR A WOMAN ..." "My poor dear husband is really broke up over that. He's still locked in the bathroom crying."

"...THE SPARKLING CLEANER ..." "Must you talk about a toilet bowl cleaner while we're eating breakfast?"

"...YOU'LL GET MORE OUT OF DUSTING ..." "If you believe that honey, why don't you come over and dust the six rooms of furniture I still have to do this morning."

"...NEW! IMPROVED ...!" "Now really, all they changed were the box and color of the label. It still taste like—*(bleep!)*"

"...THIRTY PERCENT CLEANER ..." "I'm a Math teacher. You guys like to send me a copy of the formula used to arrive at that figure please!"

"... "THEY WON'T LAST LONG ..." "Let me get this straight, you mean at those prices they'll fall apart when you get them home?"

"...YOUR RESPONSE WAS SOBERING ..." "Do you mean the store owner was drunk?"

"...REACH OUT AND TOUCH SOMEONE ..."

"Hummmmmm, say honey if you're interested I live at—!"

🎧 🎧 🎧

One disc jockey grumbled, "I can't figure out what makes listeners respond to something that insults their intelligence?"

COMMERCIAL: "HELLO OUT THERE IN RADIO-LAND EVERY-ONE. I AM HEN-RAY ROUND, OWNER AND OPERATE-TOR OF ROUND TIRE STORES. WE ARE LOCATED ALL OVER THIS HERE CITY TO SERVIE YOU THE PEOPLE IN THE PUBLIC. IF YOU GOT A FLAT AND YOU THINK YOUR POCK-ET BOOK IS FLAT TOO AND YOU SURE 'NUFF CAN'T A-FORD NEW TIRES FOR YOUR AH-TOE-MOW-BILL, THEN ALL YOU AIN'T TALKED TO ME OR MY SONS, JEFF, BIFF AND RIFF. WE ARE ALL OUT TO NEARLY GIVE OUR TIRES AWAY, WE SELL. REMEMBER, OUR MOTTO IS ... 'IF IT GOES ROUND, IT IS PROBABLY A ROUND TIRE, HA HA. USE OUR PAY AS YOU PLAY-A-ROUND CREDIT PLAN. REMEMBER FOLKS, ROUND TIRES ARE AROUND TO KEEP YOUR WORLD GOING A-ROUND!"

"Think that is a little far out, huh" says the disc jockey. "It's true, this guy has been voicing his own commercials for years, pays top dollar and know what? He's a self-made millionaire! Yet, if I'm reading someone's commercial and screw up one word, mispronounce one name on the air, the client calls my boss and complains. In some cases they want a 'make-good' commercial for free. All I get is the shaft and ass chewing. It just ain't, uh ... isn't fair."

🎧 🎧 🎧

COMMERCIAL: "FOR FINE FURNITURE ... IT'S RANDALL'S!"
The DJ started another song. Looking over he could see the

blink of the request line ringing. He frowned. For over a week he had dreaded answering the phone. He hoped that whoever was calling wouldn't' be that ... that—

"God damn it!" the voice on the other end of the receiver started, "I've told you I don't know how many times to quit running that commercial! You son-of-a-bitch, all that Randall's sells is junk! Junk, you shit's!"

The irate voice on the line would cuss some more, then hang up in the DJ's ear.

It happened nearly every time the radio station for Randall's Furniture store. Like other callers who would do this kind of thing, it was tolerated for the most part, considered harmless because most DJ's reasoned that, *'you can't please everyone'*.

"If you suck-o's run that bull shit Randall's one more time, I'm going to burn your #$$@% radio station down."

THAT THREAT WAS TAKEN SERIOUSLY!

Any threats like that, especially since the 9-11 disaster is considered a potential risk to life. The FBI is called in on the case because radio stations receive their license to operate from the Federal Government. A phone tap and trace was put on the line and it didn't take long to catch the menace making the calls.

He was the _owner_ of CRANDELL'S FINE FURNITURE ... a local competitor!

He did go to jail and he did pay a large fine!

ဂ ဂ ဂ

The **MOST OUTRAGOUS** advertisement **EVER**!

It was not on the radio but on a gas station sign across from an elementary school.

REGULAR $1.39

The service station in question had been closed for years! The current regular gas price as of today—

REGULAR $2.78

Yeah, that story is a little jab at the world we live in today, but it's more than just rising prices. This brings us to a little comparison shopping for advertising.

Headline: *"CONGRESS BANS CIGARETTE ADVERTISING ON RADIO AND TELEVISION!"*

So where did the cigarette advertising go? Try newspapers, magazines, billboards, bus and taxi signs, flying banners, etc.

Headline: *"RADIO AND TELEVISION ON ITS OWN MERIT BANS HARD LIQUOR AD'S!"*

So where did the advertising for hard liquor go?

Uh-Huh. Try newspapers, magazines, billboards, bus and taxi signs, and so on.

Headline: *"TEENAGER KILLS FOUR IN DRUNKEN HIGHWAY CRASH!"*

The newspaper story went on to say the fifteen-year old boy had chugged down seven beers claiming, "I can get as drunk on beer as I can on hard booze. After all, booze is booze!"

(By the way, there was a whisky advertisement on the same page as that tragic news story!)

Or ... how many under seventeen year olds have you seen watching R-rated movies?

Or ... have you ever been in an R-rated movie and seen a family with three very young children also watching the violence, sex and foul language oozing off the screen?

Or ... how can anyone be so angry they have the word 'FU_ K' tattooed right across their forehead?

Or ... did you know the government has been whispering a lot lately about the language in some of today's songs. Is there talk of laws to classify who can listen to what?

I can hear it now ...

DISC JOCKEY *"THERE YOU GO ... THAT LAST SONG WAS RATED—'NB' FOR ... 'NOT BAD.' WE THOUGHT ABOUT PLAYING ONE RATED 'OM' FOR 'OLD MAIDS' BUT ... INSTEAD, WE GONNA HIT YOU WITH THIS ONE RATED 'RRR' OR ... 'R3' FOR, RANCHY, RANK AND REPLUSIVE. PLEASE, GET YOUR KIDS INTO ANOTHER ROOM BEFORE THIS SONG COMES ON THE AIR!"*

Bans, restrictions, warnings, blah and blah, they're out there. But who gave the kids all those communication goodies? Parents did! So say hey, when was the last time you really knew what your kids were listening to and watching?

Still, it's all out there in the free or almost free airwaves. Remember that ban on liquor in the roaring twenties? That really worked ... right?

Gad, keep an eye out for that junior senator about to try and gain publicity beating on the banning bucket and ... who knows what the government is planning to take away in our future.

Wait! Do I hear the distant wailing of sirens?

Better not hear them on the radio though, because a few years back a radio station used the sound effect of a siren in a commercial to draw attention to something they were selling.

One lady driving along heard the sirens and not realizing they were coming out of her radio stomped on the car's brakes right in the middle of an intersection.

The results were a three car pile-up that sent five people to the hospital!

After the young woman got out of the hospital, she sued the

radio station that had run the commercial with a siren and won a healthy sum of money.

There are a lot of other things you really shouldn't hear of the radio—though in most cases, no laws have been passed banning them. Things like, fortune tellers, abortion clinics, dating clubs, strip joints, XXX rated products-like movies and 'adult toys', massage parlors, diet pills, other non-FDA pitches and more. There are a lot of *'grey'* areas when you get into some of these products.

A lot of radio stations have banned many of those products mentioned above because of **THE NATIONAL ASSOCIATIION OF BROADCASTERS**. To be a member; there is a 'code of ethics of responsible adverting' guide lines for member radio and television stations.

Like one broadcaster said. "If you don't like it, turn it off!" Ouch!

🎧 🎧 🎧

Do you remember the late comedian, George Carlin?

He recorded a skit called, *"SEVEN DIRTY WORDS YOU CAN'T SAY ON THE RADIO!"*

Sure, I can write all of those words down right now in this book—but, I sure as (blank) can't say them on-the-air!

A few radio stations have run that parody by Carlin and to this day still find themselves in court spending a ton of money to defend their rights to air the comedy bit.

Late breaking word is the Federal Communication Commission (FCC) just might be crumbling on this ban!

Have you noticed that TV writers are already trying to make sure that— *'Bitch, Butt, Crap, Hell, Son of a Bitch, pee, piss, screw you, bastard,* and others words are starting to creep into their comedy sitcom scripts? Hummmmm?

So you ask ... Donahue have you ever said any of those _'words'_ on the radio?

"ARE YOU A SHITTER BUG ... UH ... SHUTTERBUG!"

"HERE'S ONE OF DOLLY PARTON'S GREATEST TIT'S—UH, HITS!"

(Hey, I'm only human!)

I admit though, I did hear a DJ say recently on the radio; _"There you are sitting in traffic on your dead butt scratching your ass!"_

CHAPTER 6

"Now ... Live and In Person!"

"**H**ere **IT** comes, right out of that little talking box. Look! It's more than a mouth that moves, it walks and it's got arms and legs. Look at those eyes, they blink and wink! See that cheesy smile. *It's a real, live Disc Jockey!*"

It's true, you don't see them making public appearances as much as they used to do, but they still show up at Grand Opening, Bars, Car Dealer Showrooms, Movie Premiers, Malls, Concerts, Dances, Schools, Beaches, Amusement Parks, Civic Clubs, Furniture Stores, Ball Games, Rodeos, Service Station Openings, and fifteen thousand and thirty-nine other places where crowds might gather.

"Yes it is true," one DJ told me, "I once did a public appearance at a Funeral Home! Honest to God, we were pricing caskets and cost of funerals."

Did anyone show up?

"Sure did, five people came in to get a free hot dog and a new calendar."

RADIO'S REMARKABLE LISTENERS! The DJ Diaries ... has compiled a list of **ACTUAL ANSWERS** *made by listeners upon seeing a disc jockey IN PERSON for the FIRST TIME!!*

1: "You don't look like a DJ. Listening to you I thought you'd be ...
   (a) TALLER
   (b) SHORTER
   (c) BALD
   (d) SKINNY
   (e) WEIRDER
   (f) HANDSOME

2: "You don't look like a DJ. You remind me more of ...
   a) My Mailman
   b) A used car salesman
   c) My teacher
   d) A shoe salesman
   e) My Ex ...
   f) Brad Pitt ... (Sure, we wish!)

3: "Say, Mr. DJ ... can I say something on the radio. Can I?"
4: "Don't stick that thing (microphone) in my face! If you do I won't talk. I mean it."
5: "This is my little girl; she is the best ever, her tap dancing is real good. Can you get her on a record? Honey, dance for the DJ."
6: "Say young fella, I got this here song I writ back in 1953. It's a great song about World War Two. I want you to give it to one of them famous stars to sing. Okay?"
7: "I drove thirty miles to see you in person, now give me something free."

8: "Quick, take this piece of paper; I got to be careful, my husband is here with me. No, dummy, don't look over there! That's where he's standing. Listen, if you fool around, my numbers on the paper call me later ... he won't be home!"

Sometimes things a DJ says on the air can come back to haunt them when they do an in-person appearance.

"I'd just come back from a two-week vacation and the first evening back I had to make an appearance as Master of Ceremonies at a live rock concert.

The auditorium lights dimmed, the spotlight came on and the disc jockey walked out on stage and brought on the first act. All was going fine till ...

"The next band was a little slow at setting up. So, I went out and told a couple of jokes, then explained to the audience that the show would rock-and-roll in a little bit."

The disc jockey then said ...

"Hey, be cool, just hold your taters!"

As soon as he said those words, the lights above the audience blinked on, everyone stood up and held up a **POTATO!**

"Boy, I'd been had! The joke was on me. It seemed that a couple of listeners were talking one day while I was on vacation on how I often got hung up on that trite saying. They got the idea, talked the station into the idea of everyone bringing a potato to the concert. So, everyone was ready for me to say the words. I heard more laughing from behind me and turned to see everyone in the band also holding up a potato."

Listeners had brought over *four thousand potatoes!*

"After the concert all I could think about as everyone came

by the stage to drop off their potatoes was, 'how many ways can you fix a potato?'"

The next day as a public service to the community I donated most of the spuds to a couple of soup kitchens. Even a few days after than some listeners dropped off potato soup, potato salads, baked spuds, fried spuds and more.

"Phew, it made quite an impression on me because for a while, I stuttered every time I came close to saying ... 'hold your tater's!' I nearly bit my lip off several times. Hey, if I'd only had the saying, 'hold your hundred dollar bills up,' or something similar like that instead!"

🎧 🎧 🎧

Now ... time out for this word from our sponsor.

"FRIENDS ... HOW ABOUT A BIG GLASS OF ICE COLD, THIRST QUENCHING, LIP-SMACKING GOOD, TASTY AND TANGY, MOUTHFULL OF BUTTERMILK? IT'S MOOOOOOLICIOUS!"

Gad! That suggestion sure screwed up a lot of faces.

I have always loved buttermilk, especially the kind you had to churn yourself. I wore many a blister on my little hands plunging the old wooden plunger in my great-grandmothers churn until fresh cow's milk turned into butter fat flakes that were skimmed off to make butter. What remained was buttermilk.

In the years that followed, drinking buttermilk became a part of a little *'shock treatment'* when listeners watching me mouth's puckered up as they watched me chug it while doing a broadcast from some live in-person location. My on-the-air nickname became, *'Buttermilk.'* It was sort of my, *'publicity gimmick.'*

Making a personal appearance one night at a crowded bar, it wasn't unusual to have a heckler or two in the crowd. This is something DJ's become accustomed to knowing that, "hey, there's always someone out there that wants attention, especially if alcohol spirits are involved.

That night the heckler was a very inebriated lady. Loud, crass, offensive, cussing nearly every other word, she was pretty much irritating the customers, and beginning to get a little under my skin.

"Okay, we got some radio t-shirts, CD's and movie passes to give out to the next group who joins me on stage." "How about you and you ..." I started, "and—"

... and me, me, me ... you dumb shit, I can b—(hic) beat em' all, come on you, you ... ass ho—"

"Ooookay, yes, you too," I motioned the drunk lady to come up on the stage. "Watch you're ... oooops—"(she stumbled on the stairs, but crawled on up the stage).

"Yaaaa ... hey, (hic) ... HELLO!!" She screamed into a microphone.

Maybe this wasn't a good idea.

"Okay, here is how this contest works. The first place winner will get the movie passes AND then get to come back here to Happy Harper's Saloon for an evening of food and fun, drinks included. The rest get CD's and radio T-shirts."

"I'm gooooing to win that fu, fuuuu ... first place for (hic) su-su-sure," the drunken lady slurred, swaying from side to side, bumping the microphone and microphone stand.

BANG! BONK! EEEEEEEEEEEEEHHHEEEEHEHEHHE!!!!

It just had to happen, her microphone stand and mike bounced twice on the floor making an awful racket over the public address system.

The audience cringed. Oh, wonderful.

"Oh ... honey, don't bother with that ... here," I smiled reaching into a cooler. "Here's how this works," I handed her a pint of buttermilk. "On my mark of go, the first to chug this moooolicious beverage win."

One other guy in the line simply shook his head, handed me back the buttermilk and stepped off the stage. True, some people would not drink buttermilk for anything! I'd done this contest many times.

"Well, dick-he-(hic) head, dickhead, we gonna play this sssstupid game or wa-wa-(hic) what?"

"Go!" I blew a whistle and the great buttermilk chug was on. The noise the bar increased as the crowd started clapping and urging on the contestants.

A couple of contestants were slowly sipping. One's face was puckered up like he was eating a sour lemon; the other was trying hard, but was looking at the buttermilk carton more than drinking from it.

"GAAA! GAAAAHHH! GLUCK!"

All heads swiveled in the direction of the intoxicated woman. She was trying to chug, the white, slippery, slimy, stuff.

"GAAAA!" she gagged once. "GAAA!" twice.

"Uh, folks ... you might want to abandon the front row," I quickly suggested.

"GAAAAAAAAAAAAAA!" She gagged a third time.

Then she hurled! Chunks of who-knows-what, mixed with the buttermilk blew everywhere. People on the front row were falling over chairs and tables to get out of the way.

I looked around and another one of the contestants was beginning to turn as pale as ... uh, buttermilk. He too threw up. Then the lady thrashed past me waving her arms wildly in all directions, as she made a beeline in the direction of the ladies restroom.

"Hey, look at that!" A bar patron was pointing at another person on the stage. The contestant was holding his empty carton of buttermilk over his head and doing a little dance.

"Yes sir, we've got a winner."

Later, I was talking with a few customers, when one pointed

out that the drunken lady had come out of the restroom and was sitting at a table in the back. I glanced over and she was glaring at me. It was almost as if she was trying to stare a hole in me.

As the evening progressed, I'd look over every so often and sure enough, she was still fixated on me. Maybe she was hoping I would either catch on fire or puff up and blow up!

A few in the bar slapped me on the back and congratulated me for finally shutting up the old biddy. The rest of the evening went okay; I got on stage a couple more times, and every so often looked at her sitting in the back of the bar. She never said another word.

The next day she called me and poured out her embarrassment over the drinking incident and was very apologetic. I sent her a couple of movie passes.

Then a month or so passed and she called me again, sounding very happy. She told me after the buttermilk thing, she couldn't seem to get her mind or mouth to open up for booze. She'd quit drinking for good!

Wow, I can see it now …

"INTRODUCING, THE MARVELOUS MIRACLE MILK … BUTTERMILK!"

Uh, you don't see it that way?

Here are some REAL 'IN-PERSON' appearances that have not gone well for a few DJ's—

"I WAS SUPPOSED TO ANNOUNCE A MUD WRESTLING MATCH BETWEEN SEVERAL GIRLS. THEY ENDED UP PULLING ME INTO THE GOOP WITH THEM!"

"For a rodeo promotional gimmick, they were supposed to strap me on a donkey. The cowboys pulled a fast one on me and dragged me screaming like a crazy man and put me on a real mean-ass, snorting, and twisting, kicking, brahma bull! Out of the chute, I lasted one buck and shot off up into the air like a rocket, everyone got a real laugh. I got a picture of it at home, and in the photo the expression on my face is ... 'I am gonna die!'"

"I ANNOUNCED AT AN AIR SHOW AND DURING THE SHOW, SOME FLIGHT MECHANICS GRABBED ME AND FORCED ME INTO A STUNT PLANE. WE ENDED UP DOING LOOP-DE-LOOPS. JESUS, I THREW UP ON EVERYTHING!"

"I was in a watercraft race. Hell, I couldn't get up out of the water onto the thing. The machine dragged me around the water course with me hanging on the handlebars for dear life. Then as fate would have it as that damn machine dragged me by the grandstands ... *I LOST MY SWIM TRUNKS!"*

"WE ALL DRESSED IN MONSTER COSTUMES FOR HALLOWEEEN AND APEARED AT THIS 'HAUNTED HOUSE.' I GUESS THAT I ACCIDENTLY FRIGHTENED ONE KID SO BAD SHE KICKED ME RIGHT SQUARE IN YOU-KNOW-WHERE AND WHATS!"

"I was in a snowmobile race. I skidded out of control, crashed through a haystack guard rail

and into the side of a building. I broke an arm
and lost two teeth!"

*"WE SKATED AGAINST A WOMAN'S ROLLER
DERBY TEAM. EARLIER, THEY AGREED THEY'D,
'TAKE IT EASY ON US.' BUT SOMEHOW THINGS
GOT OUT OF CONTROL. ONE OF THE DJ'S GOT
HIS TRUNKS PULLED DOWN RIGHT IN FRONT
OF EVERYONE. I GOT PUSHED THROUGH THE
GUARD RAILIING AND TOOK OUT THE POOR
GUY SELLING SODA POP. STILL, IT WAS NICE
FOR THEM TO BRING FLOWERS WHEN THEY
VISITED ME AT THE HOSPITAL!"*

"I boasted I could outdo the most daring of
daredevils. I told my listeners I'd jump a bike
over seven cars, four buses, two airplanes and
twenty soldiers at the local racetrack. That night,
I DID IT! But, a rather large bunch of listeners
raised a little stink and chased me from the
track. You see, how it happened; I was hidden
behind the bleachers, and had the sound effects
of a mean sounding motorcycle roaring, and
then I quickly peddled a *Pee Wee Herman* type of
bicycle onto the track and as the people pointed
and focused on me ... two other guys ran on
the track and pulled down a pre-set curtain,
exposing a small ramp. I had no problems
jumping over the TOY MODELS!"

*"THE DUNK-THE-DJ BIT AT THE FAIR WAS MY
DOWNFALL. SOMEHOW, A PITCHED BALL
GOT THROUGH THE PROTECTIVE WIRE AND*

BOPPED ME RIGHT ON THE OLE BEAN! AT FIRST, EVERYBODY LAUGHED THINKING I WAS CLOWNING AROUND. THE BUBBLES HAD ALMOST STOPPED, AND I ALMOST DROWNED BEFORE THEY PULLED UP OFF THE BOTTOM OF THE TANK!

🎧 🎧 🎧

Then there was the DJ who actually talked a young girl into stripping, then covering her body with bumper-stickers with the radio stations call letters and frequency on them.

Her legal guardian sued the radio station because the girl was an under-aged teenager!

CHAPTER 7

"Happy Holidays!"

Holidays give radio stations and their air personalities hundreds—no, thousands of ways to do things for, with and to you ... their listeners. If there aren't enough holidays during the normal calendar year ... hey then, make some up!

"DAY OFF WITH PAY DAY!"
"OFFICIAL ... FREE MOVIE DAY!"
"TODAY ITS NO SCHOOL DAY!"

Last one sound's a little far out you say?

It really happened. We don't know how the radio station pulled it off, but they got the kids out of school for a day!

Wow, I can just see it now ...

"NO HOMEWORK DAY BECAUSE
WE-WILL-DO-IT-FOR-YOU-DAY!"

"NO WORK DAY BECAUSE WE-WILL-DO-YOUR-WORK-DAY!"

Yep, reality is ... radio stations have done those kinds of days too!

In fact, the last one was so popular the contest went on for weeks. The poor DJ's had to rotate the odd job picks and there were some doozies!

"Image being the pooper scooper in a commercial turkey shed for a day, gads," related one DJ.

"Try your hand at being a plumber's assistant clearing commode pipes; I got a whole new perspective on why plumbers charge so much crap. What a smell, well, uh ... crap."

"Image showing up for work being told you will be the doctor for the day, and he turns out to be a proctologist! I thought they were kidding until he showed me how to put on the rubber finger glove!" The jock laughed, "You should have seen the expression on my face. They finally let me in on the joke; the radio station had set me up! I didn't really have to, uh you know ... and they didn't make me watch either! Phew"

"I thought the day at a car wash would be a snap until they put me down eight feet into a sticky-icky mud pit. I had to shovel out a weeks' worth of moldy mud. Try scooping slimy mud in a shovel and throwing it over your head out of the pit!"

Ever notice in the city here you live just how many folks become *'IRISH'* on Saint Patrick's Day!

- In one major city, listeners were invited to dress green and march in a parade sponsored by a radio station that played Irish songs during the parade. A couple of thousand listeners showed up. Even a few with green hair ... and a few with green painted bodies—but one in particular panted green and little else that didn't get too far in the parade!
- In another city the radio station threw a, 'I'm Irish!' party at an Irish pub with free *GREEN BEER!* Police had

to close the club down an hour after the parted started. More people showed up that could get in the doors.

- One radio station got a surprise when a true-blue, uh green Irish Leprechaun showed up. An interview on the air revealed the leprechaun was a retired circus 'little person.' They hired him on the spot to make appearances at schools, hospitals and nursing homes before Saint Pattie's day was over.

What holiday would you guess is a DJ's biggest pain-in-the-old ... ho, ho, ho?

That was easy enough to figure out.

Christmas time music request can make a DJ feel ready for, 'ye ole rubber room!'

Like how many times can you play, *JINGLE BELLS'* or *'SANTA CLAUS IS COMING TO TOWN!'*

Think of it the DJ's way. There are maybe a hundred or so Christmas songs. Try it, make a list. Then consider this; there're maybe five or six hundred versions of those hundred or so songs.

Sure, there are some real classics—*'WHITE CHRISTMAS'* and such but ... after sitting in that radio control room playing them on the radio for hours and hours ... and *'I'M DREAMING OF A WHITE CHRISTMAS'* becomes ... 'I'm dreaming of Christmas to be over!'

Don't get the wrong impression. Disc Jockeys *DO* enjoy the Christmas season. Especially after we get out of all the, 'buy this gift, give this thing, your kid will want' ... advertisings!

We must admit it is a real challenge of trying mix and play the thirty versions of, *'WHITE CHRISTMAS'* without getting each version to close to the other version.

But no matter how hard the poor Disc Jockey tries ...

LISTENER ON PHONE: "HOW MANY MORE TIMES ARE YOU GOING TO PLAY ALL THAT SAME SEASONAL SHIT!"

The DJ had tried to be nice to the guy and agreed somewhat. But on the other hand, it *was* Christmas and he *did* have kids' of his own at home.

Reality was, there were more nice callers, especially the excited young children who—for the first time, were hearing those great old Christmas classics that even the DJ had grown up listening too on the radio.

But the scrooge wouldn't give up. He called back four or five time an hour for a couple of hours. Finally, the DJ had taken enough. He turned on the microphone and on the air said ...

"TONIGHT, WE HAVE GOT A REAL, REAL, CRANKY, CRUMMY CHRISTMAS CALLER. TRULY, HE IS A TRUE BLUE, HUM-BUG-TO-THE-SOUNDS-OF-THE-SEASON SCROOGE. HE SEEMS TO HATE CHRISTMAS MUSIC AND I THINK AT THIS TIME EVERYONE SHOULD KNNOW, ALL I HAVE GOT TO SAY TO MR. CHRISTMAS COMPLAINER IS ...

DEAR

MR. HUMBUG ...

... MAY YOUR MISTLETOE MILDEW.

... MAY A DISEASED GOOSE ROOST IN YOUR TREE.

... MAY YOUR CHRISTMAS STOCKING GET ATHLETES FOOT.

... AND MAY A TWO-HUMPED CAMEL

SIT ON YOUR ORNAMENTS!"

The Disc Jockey got a lot of follow-up calls saying, "right on!" and other nice things.

Then the DJ was nearly speechless when Mr. Humbug called back and apologized. As they talked, the DJ discovered that the elderly man was sitting alone at home confined to a wheel chair. He had no relatives left to enjoy the holiday.

Finally, when he hung up, the DJ quickly called the *Salvation Army*.

The gentleman had a wonderful Christmas!

I did too!

VETRANS DAY ... ARMED FORCES DAY ... MEMORIAL DAY ... the many holidays we need to pause and remember ... those who have fought for the freedom to enjoy a holiday day off.

But some forget ...

One DJ was shocked to finish his radio show, and once he stepped out of the building he worked in there was a Memorial Day parade marching by ...

Not once had he mentioned it on the air ... but it wasn't his fault. "No one called the radio station, no one told us the time of the parade, much less that there was one, no one!"

The DJ felt he had been lucky. "I'd never gone to war, but seeing such a poor turnout for this special day, I felt a deep nagging guilt." I'd seen the VFW, AMERICAN LEGION and others at the cemeteries' honoring our fallen soldiers. Hero's that should never be forgotten, and today I was ashamed to see a few of the sparse crowd, especially young kids laughing, and not even taking their ball caps off, or putting their hand over their heart in respect ... it was sad!"

He knew that so many older citizens were involved because in one way or another they or their family or friends had been touched with the story of someone who had made the ultimate sacrifice.

"I felt I had to do something."

That something was a series of stories taped by veterans or loved ones of veterans. He spent nearly a year collecting and recording those stories and played them on the air the next Memorial Day.

"Some of the stories weren't very pretty, and it wasn't easy for some of those old soldiers reliving the stupidity of mutilation and death. Some broke down while they were talking. Others' who had lost husbands or sons told of the gritty desolation of living without them.

"I played all the tapes for the boss before I put them on the air. He was somewhat wary of some of the content, but in the end he realized these stories must be told."

Yet, some were truly touched.

Like the little girl that wrote me telling me about going out to a local cemetery and putting flowers on the grave that said a soldier was buried in. Looking around she said her heart hurt to see so many soldier graves. She went on to tell me that she hoped her Daddy never has to go to war.

"That letter hangs on the wall in my den to this day," the DJ said sadly. "It was from a six year old girl and I wonder did he go to war? This was about forty years ago, hell … her Father and her Son for that matter could have gone to war?" The DJ has no return address. "Sometimes I wonder, I—wonder."

At the next Veterans parade the sidewalks were packed. Both veterans' organizations honored the radio station and the DJ with certificates of appreciation.

"It was a moving gesture, a tribute I really don't think I deserved in some ways … still; you must understand what I'm trying to say. Just why in hell, must man do such stupid things like create the horrors of war?"

There is no logical answer.

I know there reaches a point where I sometimes wonder just how far some of these DJ stories told to me have been exaggerated.

DJ ON THE AIR: *"THIS FOURTH OF JULY IS GOING TO BE FIRECRACKER HOT AND U U U RADIO IS GOINNG TO BE OUT TO COOL YOU OFF ... WITH OUR 'KEEP IT COOL' CONTEST! OUR GRAND PRIZE WILL BE AN AIR CONDITIONER, WITH RUNNER'S UP GETTING A GALLON OF ICE CREAM. TO ENTER HERE'S ALL YOU DO. SIMPLY SEND US A PHOTO OF YOU BEST IDEA ON HOT TO 'KEEP IT COOL' DURING THE FOURTH OF JULY!"*

The winning ideas were pretty tame when you compare them to what some other **'remarkable'** listener's pictures looked like.

1. A *nude* man reclining on a large block of ice!
2. A *bare pair of people*, lying in a DEEP FREEZE!
3. A woman with three battery-operated fans placed in uh ... uh, how do you say, *'strategic places'*!
4. A Polaroid picture of a man with a brown paper sack over his head and his ... OMG ... (True) stuck in a half-gallon ice cream container!
5. A nude woman reclining in a bathtub of ice-cubes!
6. A bare butt senior citizen standing in front of a block of ice with an electric fan blowing from behind the ice!

Exaggerated, well friends and neighbors, I saw the pictures!

The winning picture though wasn't anything like those kinds of pictures. The winner's picture showed a listeners floating in a small rubber raft in his swimming pool with about five hundred blocks of ice! We venture to say, it probably cost as much for him to rig the ice in the pool stunt as the grand prize air conditioner cost, or more!

🎧 🎧 🎧

In the early days of Mother's and Father's Day contest before cell phones, and unlimited calling plans the following happened ...

DISK JOCKEY: *"WINNERS OF OUR MOTHERS DAY CONTEST WILL GET TO MAKE LONG DISTANCE CALLS TO THEIR MOTHERS. TO ENTER SIMPLY WRITE AND TELL US WHY YOU'D LIKE TO TALK TO YOUR MOM ON MOTHER'S DAY."*

There were as always some pretty good, heart-warming winners. Like people that hadn't talked to their Mothers in years, and those that couldn't afford long distance calls, and so on.

"Winners of the contest were told to charge their long distance call to our telephone number. That way, we'd be covered in paying the phone bill," the DJ said.

But one wining listener caught the radio station off guard. He called his Mother in *Italy*, then a friend in *Spain*! If that wasn't enough ... he let his friends charge the calls they made to their Mothers, also out of the country!

When the phone bill arrived, the radio station manager wasn't ready for Ma Bell's charges.

"The charges came to about *nine hundred dollars*! The boss nearly had a stroke."

The listener was no dummy, upon getting a call from the radio station manager, he promptly explained that his lawyer said the radio never specified one call, or to where the limitations of the call could be made too, or the length of how long the conversation could be.

That's why today, if you hear that type of contest, you can bet your telephone you'll a total disclaimer ...

"WINNERS, LIMIT ONE CALL PER LISTENER, THREE MINUTES DURATION, ANYWHERE IN THE CONTINENTAL UNITED STATES!"

With cell phones and phone plans of today, talk is so cheap that type of contest has nearly disappeared.

Sometimes today's disclaimers seem longer than the contest information. As well as the announcer seems to switch into 'super speed talk' and rattle off all the rules in two seconds! But it's legal never-the-less.

🎧 🎧 🎧

Radio is or was SO creative? Take your pick.

Image a radio station on Thanksgiving doing this—

"THIS HOLIDAY ENJOY THANKSGIVING THE WAY THE PILGRIMS DID, AS WE GIVEAWAY ... A MAYFLOWER THANKSGIVING!"

The winning families got a full turkey feast with all the trimmings served by period dressed pilgrims and Indians in *MAYFLOWER MOVING VANS!*

🎧 🎧 🎧

It was the gas crisis of 1970's, I working was in Miami.

We'd been told that our country music station wouldn't draw the kind of listeners that advertisers wanted. Give me a break! I'd heard that before, having been told same thing in Cleveland, Ohio a few months before we took a Country Music station to number one! Miami was a city, if back then you broke down the populace of where most listeners came from to settle in Miami, or about anywhere in Florida, you'd have to say ...

most came from the East Coast. Then, the East Coast had very few Country Music stations.

So, when you're told, "no hillbillies or rednecks live in Miami Beach so sorry; we aren't interested in advertising on your Country and *Western* radio station." *(Sadly most advertising agencies in the 70's were so out of touch with reality. Most didn't even realize there'd been no western music played on the radio since the 40's!)*

Our radio station figured we needed to give Miami advertisers a little ... 'Heads-up!'

So, on a set date, after plugging on the air ...

"SOMETHING ... MOST UNUSUAL ... WILL HAPPEN IN MIAMI BEACH.

THAT SOMETHING ... WILL MAKE HISTORY ... AND YOU WILL WANT

TO BE A PART OF IT."

We then launched ...

"THE GREAT FREE GASOLINE GIVEAWAY!"

Gas was scarce; it was the oil crisis of the 70's and a very limited supply existed in most areas of the country at the time. *(I'll always wonder what was in the holds of those hundreds of tanker ships anchored off Fort Lauderdale.)*

We went out and bought up the entire supply of gasoline of a service station in Miami Beach, then at a highly publicized time we announced--

"FIRST COME, FIRST SERVED, FREE GAS PUMPED TILL IT RUNS OUT ... LIMIT ... ONE FILL-UP PER VEHICLE!"

We gave the gas station location and then ...

I'd say we had a pretty good turnout. Our DJ's were decked out in White Tux's and pumping the gas as the traffic piled up!

News helicopters flew overhead taping the huge mile or

more-long lines of cars, trucks, motorcycles, you name it ... waiting to be the next at the pump. Cops were everywhere!

Image, the *FRONT PAGE* of the *MIAMI HERALD* had a full-color picture of a man filling up his $100,000 *MASERATI!*

That evening on *CBS Television*, famous newscaster *WALTER CRONKITE* even did a news story about what our radio station had done in Miami Beach!

I pretty well think the advertising community came to realize we could deliver quite an audience. Yes, our ratings skyrocketed and Country Music still flourishes today in South Florida.

Were we the first to give our **'remarkable'** listeners *FREE GASOLINE?* I don't know for sure, but I did get a few calls from other pissed off program directors in the Miami market that had the same idea but didn't beat us to the airwaves.

Like I've said, *"you can't buy that kind of advertising!"*

Some radio stations still do contest and promotions today, but unique and creative ones ... sadly, not like back then.

CHILD ON PHONE: *"Sir, would you please play, 'Santa Claus Is Coming to Town?"*

DISC JOCKEY: *"Gee kid, I'm sorry, I just played it."*

CHILD ON PHONE: *"Well, play it again or I'll have Santa come over and stomp your ass!*

--Click! Buzzzzzzzzzzz!—

CHAPTER 8

"Radio Goes to the Movies!"

Years back, long before the movie, 'Fatal Attraction,' about a possessive and jealous lover, there was a film out that struck a raw nerve with disk jockeys everywhere.

"PLAY MISTY FOR ME!"

Starring *Clint Eastwood*, who played a small town DJ who, whispering with his ... 'man with no name' kind of way or ... 'make my day' ... *(Take your choice)* voice spun the platters at a NuJazz fission mishmash sort of station that only Carmel, California would have.

Also making his directorial debut in this 1971 movie, Clint, the DJ makes the nearly fatal mistake of getting involved with one of his every night radio listener fans. *(The first broken rule of the DJ no-no's!)*

The movie title was from a song called, "Misty," by Johnny Mathis, which Clint always played every night when she requested it. *(The second broken rule of the DJ no-no's! THAT drives your regular listener's crazy hearing the same old song every night, TRUE!)*

Attracted to her silky purring voice and one thing leads to another and he takes her to his *Home* and does the mad *passionate! (DJ no-no's #3 & 4. Never take a listener to your home and never do the bouncy bed thing with a listener!)*

He then has an offer to move to a bigger city making more money as we do if we work hard. (DJ no-no's #5 ... never move away, abandon a fan listener who thinks you love her!)

That will get you ... *KILLED WITH A BUTCHER KNIFE!*

As it nearly did with big Clint in the movie until he drop kicked her through a plate glass window and ... well, you have to see the movie.

That movie spooked a lot of disc jockeys and it still makes me jumpy today. Why? Because it is a subject jocks don't like to talk about. That *UNKNOWN* percent of listeners out there in radio land who, well ... uh, see the timorous, uncertain agitation we have talking about it!

After the Eastwood movie every DJ we talked with told of receiving his or her, right her ... share of crank calls.

It for a long time was called the, *"Misty Effect,"* or ... *"Hey I had a real case of the 'ME' last night!*

One jock we knew who got the *'Misty'* calls finally cracked, quit, and left town. He even left his girlfriend behind because she had at first only been a listener on the phone, then she moved in and things were fine until he'd awakened a couple of nights in a row with her sitting in the bed watching him!"

Another told me he started getting, *'Misty'* calls at home. He started sleeping at night with a pistol under his pillow!

These examples are just a few reasons DJ' and Talk Show Host change their names, get unlisted home telephone numbers and guard their home address closer than a numbered 'Swiss Bank Account.'

In earlier days, I worked with a couple of them that went

to and from work in disguise; even the Wolfman wore them for a while!

One talk show host in California was known for saying ... "This state has more cranks, squirrels and nuts per square mile than any other state in the Union!"

One day, as he was going about his usual back and forth banter on the air—

"The show was about over when I happened to glance up through the studio window. There was a stranger standing there watching. I kept talking to the listener thinking the guy was just someone with an appointment to see somebody at the radio station."

For another couple of minutes the radio talk show went on as usual, then—

"I don't know what made me glance up from my control area behind the microphone and look over at the studio window again, but something ... a second sense or maybe it was a shadow, a movement. Anyway, for some crazy reason my skin started crawling ... the hair stood-up on the nape of my neck and ... wow, I did a double-take!"

The man watching the host was wide-eyed and mouthing something the host could not hear through the soundproof glass.

"I sure as hell understood when he pointed a forty-five pistol at me!"

The man got off three shots through the window before being wrestled to the floor and overcome by radio staffers.

"For a split-second it went blank and black, and I found myself getting up from under the control desk! Frantically, I patted my entire body down expecting to find blood," the talk show host said. "As miracle sounding as it may sound, the madman had pointed the gun right at my head and fired!"

All three bullets crashed through the studio window!

"I was lucky ... zip, zip, zip. I'll never forget that sound."

The Talk Jock really was, because most radio studios have to be soundproof; so a double pane of thick glass is used whenever a window looking into a studio is made.

"As I see it, all three bullets' penetrated the first pain of glass, but in the course of hitting the second sheet of glass cause the bullets' trajectories to glance away in different directions. They found two in a wall over my head where I sat, and the third lodged in the ceiling."

"I don't think anyone ever found out why the guy was so steamed. I know one thing for sure though ... he was out to kill me. Oh in court there was the nut crap thing about hearing voices or something, the usual loony-tunes cop out."

One thing for sure ... the Talk Show Host new security included having the windows removed and replaced with a wall, and a large security electric lock on the door.

"I even got a police department buddy to give me a quick draw holster and it's fastened under the control table where I sit. The pistol is loaded and the safety is off when I'm on ... on-the-air!"

Would he use it if necessary?

"I'll only say that isn't even debatable!"

Georgia DJ killed in home after walking in on intruder. Could the intruder have thought the guy was on the air when in reality the DJ's show was only voice tracks in a computer at the radio station?

Killer never found.

LA jazz jock shot in parking lot. Did the killer know the jock was in the radio station, and waited for him to leave the building in the early A M?

Killer never found.

🎧　🎧　🎧

Lady DJ in Ohio fails to show up to be on the air for her radio show. Police sent to her home and discover her dead, suffocated in bed. Did she know her killer? Was he or she a listener?

Killer never found.

🎧　🎧　🎧

It was almost like something out of a 'slasher' movie when a man showed up one Saturday morning swinging an ax as he entered the control room in North Dakota where a DJ was on the air.

"I had a song playing, and the second he came into the control room, I jumped up and grabbed a chair," the DJ said. "The guy wasn't drunk or anything like that, he was just plain daffy with a rage. God knows what was going through his mind as he was swinging the axe at everything near him. For a moment, I thought I'm gonna get it, and I got lucky, he stumbled and fell. When he did I pinned him to the floor with the chair and called the police."

The police got there pronto, and took the guy off for metal evaluation. Listeners didn't even know what had happened.

"I'd managed to kick the ax across the room then somehow segue way a couple of songs while I sat on him. No one ever figured out why the guy went off the deep end."

CHAPTER 9

"Here's the News and Other Views ...!"

NEWS—THE WHO IS DOING WHAT TO WHOM, WHEN AND WHERE?

We surpass all other species on terra firma in our abilities to be nosey busybodies. It may have started as simply as the cave man making grunting noises and frenziedly gesturing at the next cave over, then pointing to the T Rex that just ate his neighbor—to man's quest today into everything terra incognito and other wordy news worthy thingies'.

To better communicate with others—we have left no stones unturned. Smoke signals, telegraphs, telephones, and tell-a-lady! In the old days, it took months, sometimes years to get news of what was happening to travel from mouth to ear to another mouth to another ear and so on. Then, for years, newspapers became the best form of informing the masses until radio made it instant for everyone, then television and even the internet created instant in-your-face reporting.

Today's news is now today's split second history!

Putting news all together in a radio station falls in the hands of the news department. It can be as small as a DJ simply running to a news computer, printing out all the news he finds there, then runs back and reads it live on the air. It was and still is that way in many places called a ... *'rip and read'* operation. In years past radio stations had teletype printers that chattered nearly all the time printing out a long stream of paper you would 'rip' off the printer and tear into smaller sheets to read on the air.

Or ... with the advent of networks and all-news radio stations in some cities now, you can have studio anchors, street beat reporters in the field, political analysis reporters, stock reporters, farm, sports and weather reporters, in-the-air traffic reporters, state government reporters, Washington reporters, hunting and fishing reporters, editorial reporters, even in-depth background research reporters that will take your name, trace your family tree and provide an accurate record of how many times and when was the last time you went to the bathroom!

🎧 🎧 🎧

It will always remain **'remarkable'** to me that truth is often stranger than fiction with some news stories. I'm told this story really happened in Houston, Texas.

NEWSMAN: " ...*AND REMEMBER, 13-40 PAYS THIRTEEN DOLLARS AND FORTY CENTS FOR THE BEST NEWS TIP OF THE WEEK. WHEN YOU SEE NEWS HAPPENING, CALL TWO ONE FOUR, N-E-W-S!*"

The news tip hotline rang and the newsman answered it.

"Hello? Hello!" It was a frantic sounding woman on the line. "Is ... is this the newsman?"

"Yes, ma'am it is. How can I—"

"Oh God ... oh my ... my dear God!" The lady screamed into the telephone, cutting the newsman off in mid-sentence. "Right behind my house, I ... I—"

"Hello? Lady, please calm down and—"

"There's this ... this man with a gun, I see him, I see, he ... he's dear God, its' awful! I think he's going to shoot this other person and ..." She starts crying.

"Lady, listen, have you called the police?"

"Called the ..." Heavens no! Not yet ... I wanted to win the money you offer for the best news tip of the week!"

All across the land today ... other radio station that still offer rewards to listeners for news tips have these stories to report.

- An irate, jilted lover calls a radio station newsroom. He is holding his ex-girlfriend and four other people hostage at gunpoint. Would his news story win the news tip award for the week?
- A little girl called and asked if her news story about her Mommy being pregnant could win the money for the best news tip?
- A farmer calls saying he has grown a giant squash, would his squash qualify for the award money?
- An elderly lady calls up complaining, saying her neighbor was making lewd advances. "How much do I win for that story, sonny?"
- A wife reports her husband is messing around with his secretary. "He gives me so little for the groceries, you see, and I really need the money."
- A man calls in telling the news person about a warehouse fire and wants the news tip money. (He is later *arrested* for starting the fire!
- Then there's the story of the newsman who after wading through ten other bogus stories ranging from UFO's to fake fire calls got a call from a small girl who said, "Sam died today, he was my pet doggie, and I name him after my Daddy's name and ..."

That newsman called the little girl's Mother back and later in the day; the entire news department presented the little girl with the news tip of the week award money ... and a new puppy!

🎧 🎧 🎧

Besides the standard journalistic rules of, 'who, what, when and where' ... used when writing a news story there exist other guidelines. One, most often tattooed on a news broadcaster's chest is ... *"NEVER ASSUME ANYTHING!*

However—since I'm not a newsperson, I *CAN ASSUME* the following story is true. Five people have told this story to me five times ... but each in five different ways! You might even ASSUME this is the classic case of 'assumptions.'

I'll tell it like the professor of Journalism at the University of Wisconsin in Madison told it to his class and me.

PROFESSOR: "A news person who thoroughly checked out the sources of his news stories was covering the scene of a tragic auto crash that had killed three people. As he walked around the grim scene of twisted medal and broken glass he made doubly sure of the facts he was gathering from the police, that the nearest of kin had been notified.

"The three people that had died in the crash had been a woman and her two children. Then, by a quirk of fate, or call it what you will, the police confirmed—as the newsman had asked for ... 'the nearest of kin notification.' What the newsman overlooked was not asking about notification of NEXT of kin. Other words, it was true she was visiting her parents in this town, but lived in another small town in the outskirts. So the HUSBAND as next of kin had not been contacted. It was that, the police in the pressure cooker atmosphere of the situation—somehow overlooked or forgot to tell the newsman."

The newsman went on the air from the wreck scene and broadcast the story.

"A short time later the newsman was quickly dispatched to another accident scene. It was a wreck involving the husband of those killed in the car crash earlier!"

The newsman had come up on that accident where police, later piecing together the story gave some creditability to a theory that the husband driving on the way to work heard the horrifying news of his wife and children's deaths on the radio. That terrible, shocking news caused him to have a heart attack and wreck his car. Two other people, including the husband were killed in that accident!

"The newsman almost quit his job!"

'HAPPY TALK' a term first used in television to give in-tube television news types a chance to show a little emotion, rather than looking fixated with a neutral expression at the television camera's eye.

In olden days, God forbid they should smile at the camera while reading about gloom, doom and mayhem. Old school changed when consultants created a television 'CHARM SCHOOL!' The client television stations entire on-the-air staffers were signed on to go through it.

Once there intensive focus was given to things like; when to blink, how to cock the head, what kind of smile to express how to use the eyebrows, always gravitate to your good side—you get the picture. Then they learned how to 'pony' between the stories with low-key banter that would enhance each personality, uh … newspersons visual appeal. Even the scenery got into the act having to match certain color palettes customized to showcase fixed and moving visuals.

Oh my ... sorry, gosh am I lulling you into the dark forces murky hole again, huh?

Well ... radio tried to soften up the newsperson too. Here's a *'happy talk'* conversation that became a regular feature.

Both the newsman and DJ were commenting back and forth after the noon newscast that it was, "sad," that they were both stuck on the air while everyone else got to go out to lunch.

The newsman kidded the DJ about his, *'brown bagging it'* lunch and the DJ ribbed the newsman about his, *'Howdy Doody'* lunch pail. In the course of the conversation, the newsman mentioned that his wife put a surprise in the pail each day—love notes and such, "so it wasn't all that bad."

That was all the DJ needed. He started a feature in which listeners were also invited to stop by and put a surprise in the newsman's *Howdy Doody* lunch pail each day.

There were some really zany items listeners provided for the air team to talk about. To keep it for seeming acted or scripted, both didn't know what was in the lunch pail till it was opened on the air.

There were funny cards, homemade cookies shaped like little microphones, bottles of laxative, even a ladies bra and panties!

Then one day—

DISC JOCKEY: "SAY HEY, WHAT'S TO MUNCH ON TODAY IN YOUR *HOWDY DOODY* LUNCH BUCKET?"

NEWSMAN: "UH ... LET ME SEE. WELL ... UH, I SAY IT'S ... UH, GOOD GOD, IT'S UH ..."

The newsman held up a *prophylactic*! (Condom)

DISC JOCKEY: "WELL ... MY, MY ... OH THIS IS GREAT! FOLKS, IT'S A GIANT RUBBER GLOVE FOR A CUCUMBER!"

(GOOD THING THEY WERE ON THE RADIO INSTEAD OF TELEVISION!)

CHAPTER 10

"This Portion is rated ... S - E - X!"

This chapter is hard for me to write about. Not so much because of the subject of SEX, but how listeners even some DJ's are speaking words of love crassly like crude dirty words of sex, with no feelings or love. (Trump would know something about this!)

First thing I was ever told by an 'older' disc jockey was ...

"Son, remember anytime you are in the control room, either getting ready to go on the air, or just talking to another jock remember ... WATCH YOUR LANGUAGE! Don't cuss, avoid potty mouth; you never know when THAT microphone just might be open ... and those bad words uttered will have now been heard by your listeners!"

So being in radio since I was 13 years old, I simply didn't cuss much. Even today ... I seldom use every dirty word known to man and might I add ladies too, but I'm still human and occasionally ...

Roughnecks and sailors have been pointed out to me as the worst and my Dad worked with oil field roughnecks; often taking me along when he worked. I remember many of their #$%#@X conversations. My Dad observing me one day asked, "Son, I'm rather puzzled; how come it is you don't cuss?"

I've heard many 'curse slips' on-the-air over the years, and

I've also seen and worked with some DJ's who step over the line and get sexually involved with their listeners!

Bluntly put ...

LISTENER ON PHONE TO DJ: "Hi, *honey ... oh, I'm so horny and I was wondering if we could get* together *and fuck our brains out when you get off!"*

Okay, I said the word, and SEX has been offered to me out of the clear blue sky in some situations over fifty years. That's all I will say about that.

Now here are some other DJ **'remarkable'** stories of SEX!

🎧 🎧 🎧

Here's ... Charlie C's story.

"I had the night shift and was zapping along doin' my thing on the radio. Once an hour thought, I had to read my own newscast. To get ready, I made a run to the newsroom during a record, pulled the news off the teletype machine and then beat it back to the control room. I'd usually give the news stuff a quick glance over, figuring out what I'd read, and then wait for my record to end."

At the end of the music Charlie started the news theme and commenced reading the latest news from the wires of the ... *'RADIO V T O C NEWSROOM!'*

"I'd always thought it was dumb to read news at night, who cared, all nighttime listeners wanted was music and more music, still ... the sales department sold the crap, so I had to read it. Finished, I then read the weather. It went like sort of ..."

(Charlie switched into his authoritative voice) "CURRENTLY SEVENTY-SIX OUTSIDE UNDER CLEAR SKIES ... AT ..."

(His said his eyes shifted from the news copy up to the clock on the studio wall right over the window that looked into the Newsroom)

"THE TIME IS—"

(Something in the shadows of the darkened news room moved!)

"THE TIME ... UH—"

(It moved again!)

"IS ... TEN OH FIVE AND I'M CHARLIE—"

(Suddenly, two tiny blobs seemingly pasted to the glass that separated the control room slid from side to side of the glass window in the news room!)

"...UH, CHARLIE C FOR V T O C RADIO NEWS!"

The end of the newscast had sounded pretty strange; he hoped his boss hadn't been listening.

"He had, he called and chewed me out, and when I tried to tell him something weird was going on ... he just said he'd see tomorrow and hung up in my ear."

Charlie tried to explain how those two little blobs were still on the window, he added to the explanation by trying to show how it is when the lights are off in another room and it's all dark and you can't see in and everything in the room you're in is reflected right back at you. Fact is you can't see anything in the room unless something is pressed right up against the glass.

Finally, a shook-up Charlie C jumped up, ran around the corner into the news studio and switched on the lights.

"Hi," the nude girl beamed as she turned around! "I love your show, Charlie C!"

Keeping his distance, Charlie had her put her cloths back on.

"Man, this was really, really scary. She was around fourteen year old or so no less," Charlie said, "totally nude and it has been her, uh ... her tits, that's right, 'tiny tits' pressed up against the glass that I had seen."

The girl told Charlie she didn't live that far from the radio station, had been listening to his show and as a lark, came over and found the door opened.

"Apparently, the DJ I replaced when we changed shifts forgot to lock the door. She started to cry and I had her sit down for a moment. The girl told me she was just lonely, that her parents were never home at night and, well ... she just thought this would be one way to get someone she admired to like her."

Charlie C felt it was best to simply explain to the girl that she'd experience many wonderful things in her life as she got older, but with experience comes better judgment.

"There was no sense to try and turn her over to an authority, nothing had happened. She just didn't know any better. Besides, there would be no way I'd ever try anything with a listener, much less a teenager!"

🎧 🎧 🎧

Social media has worked its way into radio big time; giving DJ's all kinds of new ways to communicate with their listeners. Most it if sort of brings back the 'DJ fan clubs that used to exist in radio, with DJ's having their own web sites or pages and it also gives new ways for listeners to make request.

But in a few instances it also opened a dark side of social media, via cell phones and computers.

"Hey baby, rack-em' up ... this is your pool boy, Doug the stick' ... doing it right, tonight with your request."

The radio station and most listeners pretty well figured the references to pool, was his love for playing billiards. Later, they found out that wasn't the case.

As Doug talked to a lot of girls and young women making request, he soon came to recognize the voices, and the requester's names, he'd eventually test the waters with each one of them until—

"Hey, bet your pretty, hey ... I got it, just text me a picture to my phone, or here's my email address."

He got a lot of takers. Then eventually the conversations lead to—

"Say, wanta join my club, it's called the rack-em up club, you hear me talk about it right? Well, it's very private; all you've got to do is shoot a picture of your breast, you know, your tits and send it to me. Ah come on, no one gonna see it but me!"

The 'stick' bit was pretty good until eventually, a parent caught her daughter taking a topless picture and after she got the story out of her, the Mom called the police.

The police set Doug up in a sting with a police woman acting as a potential picture taker and they got a warrant to search his home. They came up with hundreds of pictures of bare breasted women.

There was more. In some cases, Doug would go on after getting a topless shot to tell the woman the other part of his club.

Doug 'the stick' ... and stick wasn't in reference to a pool cue, in fact he had used his stick quite a bit, and those steamy sex pictures were also confiscated by the police.

Doug is still listed as a 'sex offender' today.

🎧　🎧　🎧

Ginny G had a sexy come-on voice, and a personality made for radio.

She's been at the Missouri radio station for about six months and had built up a good following of fans, mostly men.

She had heard all the 'war' stories that DJ's tell about getting involved with listeners, but Ginny G wasn't worried.

Then one evening when she showed up for work, she found quite a surprise waiting for her—candy and flowers.

"It was a flattering gesture. I looked at the card and all it said was ... *'from a secret admirer, that would call later.'*"

"Yes, it is … May I help you, sir?"

"Please," the voice laughed down the phone line, " …let's not be so formal. Did you enjoy the flowers I sent today?"

It was the secret admirer.

"I don't know what it was," Ginny G said, "he sounded so relaxed, uh … dreamy. To top that off, he was the perfect gentleman on the phone. He wanted to meet me but, well you know, those listener horror stories, so I said no."

They conversed for several evening. Ginny got to know everything about him.

"He said her was well educated, about the perfect age guy for me. He was athletic … so he said; laughing saying some women even called him a beautiful hunk!"

A little more curious, Ginny talked a little about herself and ask him if he could send a picture.

"I got it," Ginny says, a little-starry-eyed, remembering the picture. He was everything he said he was, tall, dark and wow, what a hunk!"

That night he called again and wanted to meet Ginny, having admitted he'd seen her recently at an on-location remote broadcast.

"He told me he thought I was beautiful, still … I put him off, saying I'd have to have a little more time. Something didn't seem right to me … I could sense something but it didn't dial in at first."

She thought about some of the previous conversations.

"I'd not given it much thought before but …" Ginny G blushed, "as the guy would be talking to me and at some point in the conversation he'd start to sound uh, sort of strained, even like he was a little out of breath and then he began talking faster and faster. My God! I couldn't believe it, the man was … *'playing with himself!'*"

End of possible love life … end of a possible relationship?

"How could I have been so dumb, how terribly, embarrassing," Ginny said, her face beet red. "Later I checked up on the guy, it apparently wasn't El Creep-O's real name or picture! How could I have been so stupid?"

🎧 🎧 🎧

One of the hardest things for a DJ to have is a friend. Really ... a *true* friend! Consider this ...

"I was working on-the-air at this radio station in a small, friendly seaside community," DJ Don B starts. "In this business when you run a contest a lot of times the losers call up and wine or say things like, '*why can't you gimmie this*' or '*you must cheat and give it to people you like* and so on."

Sometimes sore-loser listeners just simply call up and cuss the poor DJ out.

"Anyhow, one night I had this guy call me up and thank me for keeping his two kids entertained, even though they didn't win anything. I told him, I appreciated that nice thought since it was rare."

Before the call was over Don B was writing down instructions to come out to the man's home for a bar-b-cue.

"The 'Blanks' I'll call em' were a nice middle-aged couple, with two wonderful, happy teenagers, a boy seventeen and a girl fifteen," Don recalls. "It was a nice day I spent with these normal, pleasant people. They made me feel right at home. I went back several times, and even went fishing with Mr. Blank couple of times. I bowled with the family and took them out every once in a while. It was truly refreshing. Mrs. Blank was an excellent cook and good-hearted woman. We all had some good laughs. The kids treated me more like an Uncle and I enjoyed that.

A couple of months into the friendship with the Blanks things begin to change.

"I guess it took me a while to realize what was happening. You see, every so often if I had some extra concert tickets, music, or movie tickets ... I'd give them to the Blanks as a token of my friendship. Eventually, it crept up on me ... maybe it was even a little my own fault for ..." Don sighs, "After a while it no longer became a gift thing with the tickets and such. It became ... 'Why don't you have a free this?' Or ... 'why didn't you bring a free music album along, I sure want that song by so and so? Or ... 'hey, got any extra so and so, I'd like to see the group.'"

Don goes on to relate the night the friendship ended.

"The straw that broke the camel's back came one night when the fifteen year old girl and I drove down to a corner grocery store to pick up some ice."

"Don, you know that so-and-so concert is coming up, right?" He thought she was going to ask for free tickets.

"Well ... he is so cool and ..." The girl stammered, I ... I won't go all the way because I'm a virgin and, but you can play with me if ..."

"She started taking off her top," Don said. "I was almost too stunned to stop her."

"Don, please ... my boyfriend can't get enough money together to buy them and if you'd give me a couple of those tickets ... you can—!"

"Pull your top down ... now!" Don said he spoke roughly. "I couldn't believe this was happening. "I'll get you the tickets, period, stop the crap now and never offer yourself again. Damn it, you'll have those tickets tomorrow."

"Oh Don ... I'm I ... I'm sorry, please don't tell Daddy. Please."

I told her I wouldn't, I also advised her to stay away from sex till she understood a little more about life. We then drove back in silence. By the time we got back I put the incident behind me the best I could. God, I could have never done that to her, never," Don swore.

He gritted his teeth all through supper, then left and the next day after he dropped the tickets off he did his best to get past the proposition he'd been offered.

"I slowly cut back on seeing them, by telling the parents the radio station was controlling more of my time and so on ... eventually, the Blanks dropped out of my life."

Today, Don B has a few close friends ... "But for the most part I sure as shit don't tell them I'm a DJ, I just say I'm an engineer and maybe later bring the radio thing into the picture."

This is a reality of the business that some radio people experience every so often. We think it goes a long way to explain why it does seem hard for most anyone to get close to some air personalities.

"If you use my story," one jock told me, "please, please change my name. Even though I never fooled around with a listener, I was heavily tempted once. My wife is still touchy about me being a disc jockey."

Okay ... 'Harry.'

Harry was a popular air personality for several years in a very large city.

"Yeah, you get those you know ... 'let's-get-together-and-screw' calls a lot. For the most part you always knew that on the other end of the line was a poor soul. Lonely, maybe she was dejected because she's as homely as the hills and reaching for the last straw when it comes to lovers. Maybe she was an aging woman whose lover was looking for something younger.

Or maybe she was looking because her old man at home never even budged except to snore when she wanted to have sex, who knows?"

Harry had heard and seen it all. That is until one night—

"This call came in from not one, but three girls on the same line. At first, they wanted to request songs; then the gal's started asking other questions. One of them had remembered seeing me at a live concert and she told the other women I was a good looking stud."

Harry laughed, and then continued, "They started getting a little suggestive and gave some subtle hints that all of them would like me to share their bed. Get that, huh? Three babes and one guy ... something to think about!"

The trio continued to call every night for several nights. The talks got more tantalizing until ...

"Shit, I was finding it hard to keep my mind on my show. Finally, I gave in and agreed to drop by their place and see if they would dare come through with the *FUN* they all promised."

Did Harry get surprised?

"I got off work and drove over to their address, parked on the side near the side door they said would be unlocked and then went inside. It was dark except for the flickering glow of a candle I could see coming from one room."

He crept down the hall and into the candle lit room. I heard a couple of girlish giggles, a one of them whispered, 'over here Harry' and as my eyes adjusted in the low light I saw the outlines of the three girls in the same bed. But man, what I saw next ...!"

Harry had the perfect situation some men can only dream about ... except for three big problems.

"They were giggling and whispering for me to undress and join them, they were all nude and I was ready until my desire faded ... and how!" Harry exclaimed.

At three of the girls were PREGNANT! I mean watermelon size PG!

"I am not the hell sure what I said, I mumbled some excuse and got the blazes out of there."

On the outside again as he was crossing the lawn to his car he saw something he missed going in.

"It was a sign that said," Harry chuckled, "Home for Unwed Mothers!"

The story does have a happy ending for Harry.

"I nearly broke the land speed record getting home to my wife and never ... NO *NEVER* ... did I want to ever try anything like that again ... EVER!"

𝅘𝅥 𝅘𝅥 𝅘𝅥

"I've tried to remember over the years how this thing started," Larry D started, "but I draw a blank. Best I recall is this lady was working in the same building I did, maybe it was an elevator meeting or something, and hell ... she can't even remember how it happened. Somehow I wound up in her office, we talked about a little of everything and then it got off into sex pretty deep."

Larry D and the lady wound up in the supply closet and what they ended up doing was strictly triple X rated hot and horny sex.

The office supply closet affair went on for about a year.

"She'd call me and I'd drop over and we'd do things neither of us could image two people could do. She was sexy, a stunning looker and seemed we both couldn't get enough sex. She'd sometime call in the morning while I was on the air, and she was getting ready for work and we'd do hot sex on the telephone while I was on the air. It nearly drove me crazy; I could hardly wait to get over to her office later in the day. Man, we did it out at her place when her husband went hunting, and she'd even borrow a girlfriends place every so often and we'd meet."

So what makes this sexual story with a listener **'remarkable'**?

"I moved about a year into our relationship, but it didn't stop. We met in other places including Las Vegas, and by then she was divorced.

Ever see the movie, *'SAME TIME NEXT YEAR'* with *Alan Alda,* and *Ellen Burstyn,* it was about two people married to different spouses who met at an inn, and had an affair. Then for years they continued to meet every year same time, same place.

"Here's our remarkable story. We still met now and still communicate via email and it's been thirty-five years ... man, over thirty-five years! It still feels like yesterday. I guess there is a moral to my story, though you might feel I'm more immoral than moral. It's something all married couples should think about. Me, I've never remarried and maybe the problem is one peculiar to married couples. If you truly love someone, then truly abide by the vows of marriage. Agree to give your all to the marriage, work hard at pleasing your mate and this sort of thing won't happen."

Does Larry D feel any guilt?

"Why should I? In today's world the reality is, if it wasn't me, they'd find somebody else. This sort of running around exists on both sides of the bed in some of today's so-called modern marriages. I really don't understand why these types of people stay married."

Will Larry D meet the lady again?

"In a flash, it is more than just the best sex ever; it is a very compatible and comfortable situation for the both of us."

Rock'n Ron checked in with me one day and tells this story. "Meeting a lady for years is a pretty good story but ... dude, I meet eight to ten ladies a year every year and have for the last sixteen years!"

Each of them is from a different city where he was a disc jockey.

"I had an old friend who made it his passion to date only 'airline stewardesses.' It was a challenge balancing their schedules, with one flying in, one flying out, making sure his escorting one to one hotel didn't cross one path with one while with the other. This balancing act would have given any other guy a running, jerking fit."

CHAPTER 11

"Request Time Again ... With A Bonus!"

Get ready out there in radio land, dudes and dude'ett's, it's time to give us a call and request your favorite tune. Tonight ... a *BONUS*! DEDICATIONS! Right you are booby. Dedicate one to your girlfriend, your wife, your loved one, your mother-in-law, friend, fiend, zombie or even your favorite giraffe!

(These are **REMARKABLE** request made by listeners like *YOU*!)

🎧 🎧 🎧

DISC JOCKEY: "RADIO Y A C K, WHAT WOULD YOU LIKE TO HEAR?

LISTENER: "Uh, play a song for my poor dead parakeet. He died yesterday. Please, his name was Eagle."

🎧 🎧 🎧

DISC JOCKEY: "RADIO Y A C K, GOT A SONG AND DEDICATION?

LISTENER: "Yeah, play 'Messing Around,' for my fucking wife. Got that? My fucking-around wife!

𝇟 𝇟 𝇟

DISC JOCKEY: "RADIO Y A C K, HELLO, YOU GOT A REQUEST?"

LISTENER: "Yep we do, (hic) us gent-to-men down here at the Red, (hic) ... uh Red Eye Salooneee, got a, an ar—argument to sett-le. Okay de doaky? Sssss-say, what was John Fitzgerald Kennedy's middle na-na-name?

DISC JOCKEY: "SIR, FITZGERALD WAS HIS MIDDLE NAME?

LISTENER: "No da-da-(hic) damn it, we want to know his middle name you f-f-fu-(hic)-ing idiot!"

𝇟 𝇟 𝇟

DISC JOCKEY: "RADIO Y A C K, WHAT YOU GOT IN MIND?"

LISTENER: "You honey, now if I can get you to come over tonight I could—!"

𝇟 𝇟 𝇟

DISC JOCKEY: "RADIO Y A C K, GIVE ME YOUR DEDICATION."

LISTENER: "Uh, Oh! I don't know anybody, sorry, sorry!"

𝇟 𝇟 𝇟

DISC JOCKEY: "WHAT'S YOUR REQUEST AND DECICATION?"

LISTENER: "Please, would you play ... 'Crying in the Chapel" by Elvis for uh, dedicate it to ... Joan Neal Hart, okay?"

DISC JOCKEY: "SURE, J-O-A-N, NEAL HART, GOT IT DOWN, SIR."

LISTENER: "You, uh, you know ... Joanie's been dead for five years and I ... I still can't forget her, we were so—"

🎧 🎧 🎧

DISC JOCKEY: "Y A C K RADIO REQUESST LINE ... HI."

LISTENER: "Hello, uh you don't know me, but ... but, well uh, I bet you're getting a little hungry by this time and I have just baked a cake and uh, I'm going to pick up some ice cream, so I thought maybe you'd like to share a piece ..."

DISC JOCKEY: "WELL DEAR, UH ... I'M NOT REALLY SUPPOSE TO LET ANYONE INTO THE RADIO STATION AT NIGHT, BUT ... YEAH, GUESS I AM A LITTLE HUNGRY, COME ON OUT AND RING THE BELL ..."

LISTENER: "That's great, see ya ... thanks!"

🎧 🎧 🎧

DISC JOCKEY: "REQUEST LINE, RADIO Y A C K, WHAT'S YOURS?"

LISTENER: "Hi guy ... say, play "Two of a Kind" for Jim B from Rose C. Okay?

DISC JOCKEY: "NO SWEAT DEAR, OH ... GOT THE SONG RIGHT HERE, I'LL DO IT NEXT!"

The Disc Jockey proceeds to hang up, cue the next song up, turns the microphone switch on the air and says ...

"RADIO Y A C K REQUEST AND DEDICATIONS, HERE'S 'TWO OF A KIND" TO JIM B FROM ROSE C ..."

He starts the song and while it is playing he answers the next request line.

DISC JOCKEY: "RADO Y A C K, YOU GOT A REQUEST?"

LISTENER: "You son-of-a-bitch, this is Jim B, who in hell requested that song you're playing and dedicated it to me from that bitch Rose C, I ought to come out there and stomp your ass, that sucks, Rose C is the ugliest girl in school, damn you!" The Disc Jockey tries to offer an apology, and explain what happened but the listener hangs up in his ear.

He's had his limit for the evening ...

DISC JOCKEY: "HEY THERE, THAT'S ENOUGH FOR TONIGHT, HOLD YOUR CALLS, I'V GOT MORE THAN I CAN HANDLE FOR A WHILE, HOLD YOUR CALLS PLEASE." *Hell, he thinks to himself ... I'll just make up the names and such for the rest of the evening, yeah ... to hell with it.*

About that time the light and bell that signals that someone is at the locked front door goes off.

"Oh man, I got it made in the shade," the Disc Jockey halfmumbles to himself ... "Tonight, tonight after work, this sweet lady at the door with the food and I can maybe ... hummmmmm, maybe ..."

The disc jockey gets to the door, opens it and there ... ice cream, cake, and all stands the most obese, repulsive woman he has ever seen in his life!!! Well ... at lease she brought a case of beer!

(It Figures!)

THE THREE R's
The Reality of Request Radio

Today, MOST ... that's right MOST radio stations that claim to take request aren't going to like me saying this but ...

... request are a nice gimmick but, more often than not in today's radio station request are a smoke screen and what you hear is more than likely not what you're going to get.

They Simply DON'T play what you request!

1. Most radio stations today have one disc jockey in a
    satellite studio God knows only where, doing a show
    on a thousand radio stations in cities all across the USA
    at the same time. If you drove from city to city you'd
    hear ... *same jock* ... *same music*! If you call that satellite
    fed local radio station to request a song they will tell
    you ... "yeah, sure we'll get it on." Then hang up and
    do nothing ... duh! Because, **Reality of Request Radio**
    is ... *THEY ARE NOT PLAYING THE MUSIC AND NO DISC
    JOCKEY IS EVEN IN THE BUILDING!* Get it?
2. Those radio stations that *DO PLAY THEIR OWN MUSIC*
    and have their *OWN DJ's* still don't do request ninety-
    nine percent of the time because, by the time you hear
    their show on the air ... they are either doing another
    job in another room at the radio station, gone to lunch,
    or gone home. The sound live but they are recorded,
    and they don't tell you that! They have cut what is
    called, VOICE TRACKS. Taking a printed log of the songs
    ALREADY SCHEDULED in advance on the computer,
    they go into a production room and pre-cut their audio
    tracks or VOICE TRACKS, giving the title of the song,
    and other gab and info into a computer. This takes
    about an hour. When they come out ... they load those
    VOICE TRACKS into a computer that places them in the
    correct slots between the songs. That hour or so work
    the DJ has done with recorded VOICE TRACKS ... now
    can make up a whole FOUR HOUR SHOW, and they
    don't even have to be in the radio station. In some cases
    they can cut an entire WEEKS worth of shows in one
    morning. **Reality of Request Radio** is ... no live DJ ...
    no live music ... all PRE-RECORDED = No request!

3. Anytime jocks answer the phones they are briefed on how to handle listener requests with very well thought-out answers. Those are usually ...

- *"I'LL **TRY** TO GET TO IT."*
- *"MY LIST IS LONG BUT ... **IF POSSIBLE** I'LL PLAY IT."*
- *"I'M **NOT SURE** WHERE THAT ONE IS, **MAYBE** IF I FIND IT"*

Finally a lot of radio stations you hear today with music ... *DON'T EVEN HAVE A LIBRARY OF MUSIC THEY CAN PLAY IN THE ENTIRE RADIO STATION!!!* True, why should they? Many have a thirty minute computer show put together in case the satellite is off-the-air or something else. Try asking a DJ where the music you are listening right now originates from. You will be amazed how many don't know. Now that is scary!

CHAPTER 12

"The God Block"

I n radio lingo disc jockeys call it ... '*THE GOD BLOCK.*'
It is a bunch of back-to-back religious or church programs, usually pre-recorded that are on-the-air on Sunday morning's on a lot of radio stations.

It is the most *DREADED* job a DJ can have in radio. It has little to do with how religious a DJ's personal beliefs. It is usually this; He is stuck in the studio running all those shows because he's having to pay some penance for some misdeed, or because the Program Director couldn't get a *newbie radio kid* to do it.

A little more background is needed here. It matters not a DJ's religious indoctrination from childhood to what the DJ believes today. It becomes curious at first to listen to a pastor, minister, or priests explicate the gospels of how God controls and commands what we do. But eventually, after a few Sundays of hearing how each church and its teachings are they are the '*only*' true ones, or the right way and how fear and damnation are always with us ... it gets arduous to keep focused on listening.

It doesn't make him anti-religious really, it just becomes more mind bending than most can handle. Image, could YOU—say listen to ten programs in one morning, each structured with a different religious credence? Yeah, maybe for a short time, you get the picture. So the old timer DJ sits there with the sound turned down reading the Sunday funnies.

Still, some *'Old Mikes'* in this business got their start on the Sunday morning religious programs, including myself. Yes, we were those *'newbie radio kids'* that were excited just to be sitting in a radio stations control room running the church tapes. Hey, we were in real radio, with the big control console, turning the speakers up and down ... listening, to those (*do I dare say*) ... groovy *'fire and damnation'* preachers chase their flocks!

If we were really, really lucky we'd get to read the weather and then tell the listeners what radio station they were tuned in on. There we'd be rehearsing the weather and station identification call letters over and over right before our ten or fifteen seconds of fame between each church program.

Then the church program would end and the next sound that would be heard would be ...

*"THE JEWEL OF THE FOREST, THIS IS RADIO R Q B X, BLANKTOWN. IT'S SEVEN-EE, (**oh no, voice cracked**) UH, IT'S SEVENTY-SIX DEGREES."*

Wow! The *newbie radio kid* was sweating, his throat was dry and there was a funny, tingle around the lips. His ears were red, was it hot in studio?

Then it hit him ... *zip-a-de-do-da*! Hot dog, he was in radio!

His voice just went through that microphone, out of that radio building through a thing called a transmitter which that weird talking engineer tried to explain how voice was turned into squiggly waves. Well, no matter, for the *newbie radio kid* just knew hundreds, no ... thousands of people just heard his voice on the 'God Block' shift.

What power!

"Dad, Mom, did you hear me on the radio? Did you? Did you?"

"Yes son that was nice, by the way ... when you read the

weather what did you mean when you said, *'winds would be* **valuable'**? Shouldn't that have been **variable**?"

"Oh no, oh my God, Dad ... did I REALLY say THAT!"

"Yes, you did," said my Mom. "And stop that cussing!"

(*Over the radio years I've 'screwed' up worse than that.*)

"Son, you're cussing again!"

"Uh, yes ma'am."

Moms have always been able to read kids thoughts!

🎧   🎧   🎧

"We had this live show from our studio on Sunday morning called, *"In Touch With Christ,"* says CJ the DJ. "It was a program where two ministers would come in and explain their different religions on the air. Running the show was simple. I just turned on the microphones in the studio, turn down the monitor speakers I listened on in the control room, prop my feet up and read the Sunday news."

It was not unusual for a DJ to bring along a book to read like, *'War and Peace'* or something longer for a six hour run of church programs.

"I'd finished reading the newspapers news, and was in the middle of *'Dagwood'* when I glance up at the clock to make sure all was okay then I checked the preachers in the studio. Something wacky, strange was going on."

CJ watched a little stunned, as both preachers were stand up waving their arms wildly.

"It threw me at first, I mean, it looked so strange. Realizing I saw their lips moving but couldn't hear them, I quickly turned up the monitor speaker volume."

The ministers were in hot debate about something. Then all hell broke loose!

"Both guys were really tearing into each other. Their faces

were flushed and I couldn't believe what I was hearing." CJ shook his head and continued, "They were swearing at each other, then one preacher swung at the other and ... bop, bloody nose!"

Suddenly CJ the DJ remembered that this whole fiasco was going out on-the-air.

"The other minister looked stunned for a moment then he took a swing and a full blown fight was underway."

Poor CJ grabbed the first song he could find, put it on the air, and cut off the live studio program.

"I ran into the studio and finally separated them. Phew, what a crazy morning that was," CJ the DJ said, grinning!

In Touch With Christ" was canceled.

Remember the song that CJ the DJ grabbed and frantically threw on the air when he took the religious shows mayhem off the air?

"HOUSE OF THE RISING SUN," by the Rolling Stones!

We have heard several old jocks tell this story. In many cases, each swears it happened to them! (**Sssssssh, don't swear this is the religious section.**)

Used to be, long time ago, anytime a radio station was on-the-air, someone had to be on duty within the studio or transmitter facility.

That was the law back then. Now, it's different. With most stations running the operation through a computer and satellite, sometimes all religious programming and everything else, the commercials, the music ... everything is automated. You won't find a live person anywhere near much less in a radio station.

"I had sat through two hours of lackluster preachers doing

their live shows," Wayne O told us, "then after the last guy left the studio; I had several taped and record transcriptions to run. That was about the same time my stomach got the rumbles."

Wayne O knew he wasn't supposed to leave the radio station unattended but ... there was a little café down the road about a mile that had the best country ham and eggs.

"I had a one hour religious recording transcription I started and I sneaked out to that little joint knowing that I'd be back before the program was over. I'd done it before."

Wayne O was sitting on a stool enjoying his breakfast when a couple of guys came through the door laughing and talking about something they heard on the radio.

"Radio, did he say *RADIO?" Wayne O blurted out with a mouth full of eggs.*

Wayne O's ear's perked up! "I got that queasy feeling something was wrong back at the radio station."

The DJ nearly broke his neck running out to the car. Once inside he switched on the radio and heard—

"*...TO HELL* ... click!" "*GO TO HELL* ... click!" "*GO TO HELL* ... click!" "*GO TO HELL* ... click!" "*GO TO HELL* ... click!"

What Wayne O was hearing was the needle stuck in a grove of the church record transcribed program.

"*GO TO HELL* ... click!" "*GO TO HELL* ... click!"

"That little nick in the program record was about ten minutes into the program. The next weekend when the show got played back in its entirety I heard what had happened."

The preacher was saying ...

"AND IF MAN DOES NOT SHOW COMPASSION, DOES NOT REPENT, SURELY THEN HE WILL ... "*GO TO HELL* ... click!" "*GO TO HELL* ... click!" "*GO TO HELL* ... click!"

That stuck phrase must have repeated for around fifteen or so minutes that day before Wayne O got back to the radio station where his boss was waiting for him.

"Yeah, I got fired on the spot."

DJ JIM F. told us about his beginning days in radio doing the '*God Block*.'

"It was at a very small radio station, in a very small town. I was supposed to sign the radio station on for broadcast on Sunday morning's at six O'clock A. M."

Okay, image you're a *newbie radio kid*. When you were young, and away from the home nest working your first job, living alone and out of town wouldn't you party nearly all night long Saturday night?

Jim F opened an eye and focused on the alarm clock. It was *NEARLY* nine in the morning.

"It felt soooo good to sleep in until reality hit me and I realized I was about three hours late for work!"

It went downhill from that point.

"I think I ran the town's only two red lights getting to the radio station. Jumping out of the car I ran to the front door," explains Jim. "As I was unlocking the door, I heard a thud and crunching sound ... gad, I had forgotten to put the car in park. It had rolled backward and crashed into a little utility shed."

After rushing inside, he hit all the switches that turned on the transmitter. Jim F grabbed the religious tape program that was supposed to be on the air.

"I started it at about time the program would be normally be running and put it on the air."

After a couple of minutes of heavy breathing Jim F sat down and shook for a full five minutes. He was sure that if God didn't strike him dead for missing the earlier religious problems, the boss would surly fire him before the morning was over.

"Then I don't know what really made me notice but no lights

blinking on the telephone alerted me to the fact no listeners was calling in." He watched the phones for a time. "They didn't ring ... no one seemed to wonder why the radio station had begun broadcasting three hours late!"

Jim F had worked the Sunday morning shift for about six months, and it dawned on him ... "I don't ever remember getting a call at the radio station on Sunday morning ... period!" Was NO ONE listening on Sunday morning?

"No, surely not, no way, that would be harebrained?" Jim F whispered, and then smiled. "I decided to try a little experiment

Zap ... just like that, Jeff F stopped the show.

"I told myself; '*okay*' ... I'll keep Mr. Preacher here off the air till somebody ... anybody called the radio station wondering what was wrong!"

DEAD SILENCE!!!!!

"Nothing ... n-o-t-h-i-n-g," Jim F spells out. "Nada called so ... I finally felt guilty and put the show back on the air five minutes later."

Could it have been possible that there were no listeners to *THAT* Sunday morning or *ANY* Sunday morning program?

I sure don't know that else to tell you," Jim F answers the question. "I figured that the boss would eventually get a call from a listener about the late sign on or missing an earlier show. No caller period. I never told anyone about this till now. It was pretty freaky, huh?"

There are still a few live religious programs done in a radio station's studios that are complete productions. Few today are live though, most are recorded. They range from a piano player, singer, and a pastor to entire choirs, small band, even several faithful followers around to testify and be a part of the *'Amen'* section.

Here's one live religious production listeners heard.

- **PREACHER ON AIR:** "WE WANT TO THANK OUR WONDERFUL CHOIR FOR THAT BEAUTIFUL HYMN. TRULY, IT INSPIRES US TO BRING A MESSAGE THAT WILL BE OF GREAT IMPORTANCE TO OUR MANY SHUT-IN'S WHO CANNOT BE IN CHURCH TODAY. LET US PRAY ... FATHER, WE ARE—"

About that time a lady in the choir opened one eye, peeked, and then shrieked!

She was joined by other screams as everybody's eyes blinked open wide-eyed in disbelief to see a boy and a girl run into the studio. Both had paper sacks over their heads with eyeholes to see out ... and *THAT WAS ALL!*

The church program was being *STREAKED!*

There was almost indescribable bedlam in the studio.

The nude pair streaked through the band section knocking over the cymbals, the girl stopped long enough to bang a few bars on the piano. The preacher was too dumbfounded to move. At first it was hard to understand what he was saying until the cuss words started flying! Two women had dropped back down into their chairs and covered their faces with both hands, the other choir ladies continued to scream and jump up and down. Image if you can what the radio listeners were hearing.

Finally, coming to their senses the DJ and the radio stations engineer shut the program down, then managed to block the escape of the 'bare pair'! They were turned over to the police and later appeared in court. (*Fully clothed we might add.*)

It was a wise Judge that sentenced both parties to mandatory

Sunday school and church for the next two years. In addition, the sentence called for the pair to work after each service cleaning up the church.

Here's the 'remarkable' part ...

The lady listener that told me this story *was the girl that streaked*!

Even more 'remarkable' is that she is *a Sunday school teacher* today!

🎧 🎧 🎧

"How Religion Brought Me to Radio!"

Okay, my story. It all started with a church program, broadcast on a radio station.

I was growing up a typical twelve year old in a small town in Louisiana. School, games, swimming pool, fishing and exploring the junkyard were the norm. That is until I watched a small building going up about two miles out of town. Riding out each day I finally observe some men putting up a tall red and white tower and I found out it was going to be, yep ... a radio station. Hey, I had an old piece of a radio at home and if I was lucky I could even tune-in a couple of distant stations on it at night.

Some time passed and one night I was playing the radio, tuning the dial and a new signal of a radio station blared through the speaker so loudly it nearly blew me off the bed. Had to be the one I'd seen under construction just outside of town.

"Ah, Dad ... I wanta see what a radio station looks like," I said one day to my Father, "please!?"

"No not now, they are way too busy to mess with you."

More time passed, and I found myself listening to the local radio station every day. Even our church had its Sunday services and even a Sunday school show on the air."

"Hey Dad, now I don't have to go to Sunday school and church, I can just listen on the radio at home."

"Yeah, sure you can, Son."

"Hot Dog, really?"

"Yes, you could listen to those programs at home, but no, young man ... you will still go to church on Sunday."

"Oh drat!"

"Quit that cussing!"

"Yes, Mom, I'm sorry."

The Sunday school program was called, "Sunday School of the Airwaves." Each week a different Sunday school group would go out to the radio station and the class would participate in the broadcast from their studio.

The time finally came for our elementary junior Sunday school class to do the program. On the Sunday before the program, our teacher handed out slips of paper to each kid to as she put it, "memorize what is written on the paper and next Sunday you will read it on the air."

Everyone got a slip of paper; everyone got apart ... EXCEPT ME!

I was crushed! What had I done wrong? Was the teacher mad at me? Was I being punished for some awful sin I couldn't remember?

I just knew in my little mind I was a good talker because my Mom was always saying about how I rattled on, non-stop all the time around the house.

To go along with the embarrassment of not having a part to read, all the kids from the class teased and picked on me for the rest of the week at school.

This was a MAJOR crisis in my adolescent life!

Then the Sunday of the radio show rolled around.

"Come on, honey," my Mom said, as she tapped her foot, "up and out ... you're not really sick."

"Yeah, come on Son," my Dad added, "besides you know how you love listening to the radio and today you and your Sunday school class will finally get to see the inside of a radio station."

How true, if I got up and went I'd get to see inside a radio station. But how cold I overcome this humiliating boy without a part to read thing? Had I wondered ... anyone ever died of *embarrassment*?

Arriving at the little radio station, I noticed that all the other kids were showing off, bragging about how well they had memorized their parts for the broadcast. Me? I was still miffed at the Sunday school teacher for not giving me a part of my own.

The engineer ushered us into a small room that reminded me of a gold fish bowl with its soundproofed walls and glass windows were visitors to the radio station could see into the studio. On another wall another glass window looked into a strange cubicle with all the dials, blinking lights and meters.

The engineer called it the control room, and after a last minute check, he hushed the kids. Pointing to the 'on-the-air' light he then instructed each kid how to stand in front of the shiny chrome-plated microphone when it was their time to speak.

"THE SUNDAY SCHOOL OF THE AIR WAVES ... IS ON THE AIR!!!"

The voice boomed out of the studio speakers.

"YES FRIENDS, JOIN US NOW AS THE TWELVE-YEAR OLD JUNIOR BIBLE SUNDAY SCHOOL CLASS BRINGS YOU THIS MORNING'S SUNDAY SCHOOL LESSON."

I noticed that voice was coming on the other side of the glass window from a man talking into a microphone and wearing round cans on his ears. (Earphones)

This was *NEAT*!

On came the studio's on-the-air red light, and the teacher started the kids one by one toward the microphone. As each kid tiptoed up and read their line, the better each one did.

Boy, all this did was make me feel more *DEJECTED,* remembering I had *NOTHING* to say. My dejection turned into a pout when one little girl read her line, turned around and stuck out her tongue at me!

I was beginning to churn inwardly ... getting more and more agitated when suddenly ... faintly at first, I heard my Sunday school teacher saying my name for the second time—

"...*uh yes, now little Davie Donahue will give our closing prayer.*"

WHAT! I felt a tingle run up my spine! I was in awe; could I really believe my ears? Wow, my teacher considered me good enough to do something on the radio without having to read it off a piece of paper like the other kids! *Hot Dog!*

Today, I recall it vividly like a slow-motion playback in my mind.

I felt myself moving on legs of rubber toward that large shiny studio microphone. My heart seemed to have jumped up into my throat, was I a little dizzy? I reached out and lightly touched the microphone. Was there a buzzing in my ears or what? Pausing ... I looked around the room at all those faces; all those eyes riveted on me, I took a deep breath and said ...

N O T H I N G !

My mouth was moving, but nothing, no utterance; no-thing, *NOTHING* was coming out? My mind seemed to be screaming a jumble of words, yet they just wouldn't connect with my mouth!

THIS WAS A NIGHTMARE!

Out of the corner of my eye I could see the engineer in the control room jump up from his chair. He was frantically pushing buttons and looking around with a panic stricken expression. Still on the radio airwaves there was ...

... SILENCE!

The other kids begin to whisper and snicker. The Sunday school teacher looking like she could lay an egg started biting her nails

Was I in trouble? I imagined I could feel warm sweat pouring from every pore of my body. Then I realized the awful truth. I had just ... *WET MY PANTS!*

Beyond a doubt, right there in front of God and everybody in the studio I found myself standing in a growing puddle of water!

It wouldn't have been so bad if I'd left it at that ... but at about the same time my *'mike fright'** wore off I blurted out for the entire listening audience to hear—

"OH, GOD! I JUST PEE'D MY PANTS!"

End of broadcast, but not the end of this story.

*If you're ever had to talk in front of a crowd for the first time, it's called *'stage fright,'* or if you've had had a microphone shoved in your face you might understand on that Sunday morning I was having a case of ... *'MIKE FRIGHT!'* It doesn't happen to everyone but there are thousands of loopy, dumb bunny reasons you could write another book about why people freeze up.

I thought I'd never live down that experience and at times to this day I remember my Dad would say in later years ...

"Say Son," my Dad would kid, "did you pee your pants when you interviewed *Clint Eastwood*?"

"Yeah, you got it ... Ha ha, very funny, Dad."

I guess that Sunday morning back in the fifties made me a

little crazy. I had to beat that dumb, shiny hunk of metal called a microphone.

I became obsessed.

Now, as they say in radio ...

"STAND-BY EVERYONE ... TO READ HOW A TEENAGER TURNED INTO THE KILIOCYCLE KID, TO RIDE THE RADIO AIR WAVES ALL ACROSS THE LAND, AND MEET THE MOST REMARKABLE RADIO LISTENERS. THE FACTS, THE TRUTH, THE EXCITING DRAMA NEXT! But first folks, we have a word or two or three from our sponsors!"

CUE THE PLUG:

Stepping out of my official writer/author/DJ kinda thing I'd like to pass this on to you.

"THE DJ'S DIARIES; RADIO'S REMARKABLE LISTENERS" is just what it says ...

"If you have **EVER** turned on a radio ... **THIS BOOK** might be about **YOU!**"

The reactions so far with this first book are *ALREADY* generating listeners visiting my website to me to tell me of how they have been involved with a DJ (them deejays, Disc Jockeys!). So we find ourselves already working on a sequel to The DJ DIARIES ... *Volume Two.*

A lot of past radio personalities I haven't talked with in years and other people in the media's surrounding broadcasting business are sending their stories of involvements with listeners. (Like YOU!) (Media types like television people, networks, advertising agencies, syndicated radio shows, and more.)

Epilogue: "Radio ... I Did It My Way!"

"Hum a few bars and I'll see if ..." Oh, never mind. After my embarrassment in front of my Sunday school class in that little radio studio in Louisiana ... I somehow knew what I wanted to be for the rest of my live.

I became obsessed; I wanted to be a disk Jockey!

"Son, you're only twelve years old," my Dad said, "you'll change your mind a hundred times about what you want to be before you get out of high school, you'll see."

At twelve years old I built my first radio station.

A spare closet under the staircase served as my studio. You have to start somewhere ... really! I had an almost useless record player; two worn out phonograph needles and several scratchy *Glen Miller* records my parents had thrown away. Garbage cans from every alley became my hunting grounds for old radios and anything that looked like a radio part, broken or not.

The microphone, that ghastly thing that so stunned me speechless and gave me a bad case of '*mike fright*' was made out of a tin can, with the label stripped off. Punching a hundred holes in it with an ice pick, and taping it to a sawed-off broom stick and I had a microphone. Later, my first real microphone was an old army crystal element powered thing incased in black plastic. The tin can sounded better.

Every day after school I would close myself off in that

closet and mimic every disk jockey I'd heard on the radio. On weekends I'd pedal my bike two miles out to that little radio station in the cow pasture for a visit.

Boy, did they have pegged ... For free, I swept and vacuumed the studio, control room and offices and they gave me *'finders' keepers'* on everything I could take from the trash cans. All the old news copy, radio advertising copy, old records (disk), burnt out radio tubes, and electronic *zibble-witches*, which is what the engineer called anything he didn't want to explain to me.

"Kid ... it's a zibble-witch, and a purple one at that. It is a switch that remotely connects zibble tang to the perpendicular switch on-E, not off-E that one is yellow. Okay? Don't me any more questions; I'm busy drawing up electronic diagrams to defuse the transport kibble magnetic conductor plate. It's dangerous to talk right now."

Gazooks! I knew I didn't want to become an engineer. But surprise, in a few more years I did become a Radio Telephone Federal Communications Electronic Engineer.

Why?

I had to learn about all that zibble-witch stuff just to be qualified to flick on one switch and push two electronic buttons to change the direction of the radio stations signal. Why? Uh, forget about it, it's not important, *'It's dangerous to talk right now about it.'*

Not long after I read my very first weather forecast on the air but not before they had me rehearse it fifty times before I did it live.

After that I was an official *newbie radio kid* with my first job. I was paid twenty-five cents an hour. Wow!

What a fabulous job it was! I cleaned up all the radio station then spent six hours running the ... *GOD BLOCK!*

Kinda figures, huh?

But way off in the distance through the crackle and pop of the static a new sound was radiating from radios everywhere.

It was the early fifties ... and *ROCK N' ROLL* was getting louder and louder. Adults didn't like it but teenagers were going nuts!

I was a teenager that became THAT kilocycle kid riding the rock n' roll radio range!

- **EDITORS NOTE:** *IN 2000, DAVE DONAHUE WAS INDUCTED INTO THE COUNTRY MUSIC DISC JOCKEY HALL OF FAME DURING CEREMONIES IN NASHVILLE, TENNESSEE.*

BROADCASTING BUZZ WORDS:
Dictionary of Definitions

'*AMPLITUDE MODULATED*' to '*ZIBBLE-WITCH*' ... broadcasting has a language all its own. Words that to a DJ are simple, but the listener *might* not understand. Like ...

"Run the next cart in cue, make mike one audition for talkback and set tape three pot gain up for air, then listen down the line for the ten second start tone."

You get the idea. Thus, we offer the best description's we can so the next time you *TRY* to communicate with a disk ... uh, record, cart, LP spinning' jock, deejay, disc dude, air personality or *shudder* radio engineer, you may understand them or go crazy. Good luck.

Our apologies to the fine folks who put together real dictionaries!

🎧 🎧 🎧

- **AFTER COMPUTERS:** Also defined as (AC*). Most radio stations use computers today that run just about everything including, the disc jockeys, music and commercials. Things run smoothly and perfect without human intervention ... with out—without—without-without—without—without ... (*please call engineer!!!*)
- **AIR:** What the DJ expels, but seldom inhales.

- **AIR HEAD:** A $%#&!* listener or a $%#&!* Disc Jockey!
- **AIR WAVES:** DJ's words that are turned into squiggly squirms of electronic stuff you can't see, but are magically transmitted to your radio, false teeth, pacemaker, computer or microwave. (*See broadcast, see transmit, see weird engineer.*)
- **AIR PERSONALITY:** Usually live human on-the-air or recorded human that has ability to do more in ten seconds than just tell you every so often what music artist is being played, and maybe try to make a funny joke about something, maybe the engineer. (*see Disc/disk Jockey, DJ and such, see announcer*)
- **ANNOUNCER:** One who announces, declares, proclaims to say, to make known all things, known and unknown. To announce music titles of the disk, (*see disc or disk*) to act as host of, to be master of ceremonies of, (*see MC*) introduces radio programs, announce time, weather and other stuff that you want and don't want to hear. (*see commercial, see spot*)
- **AMPITUED MODULATED:** Also called A. M. radio. (sic) It is very different from F. M. (*see Frequency Modulated. See engineer again!*)
- **ANTENNA:** An arrangement of wires, rods, towers, used in sending out and receiving electronic waves. (*See air waves. Don't see engineer ... he will try to explain this crap and only confuse you more!*)
- **AUDITION:** Term used by DJ to listen to something before he/she broadcasts it and makes a bad boo-boo! (*See Cue/Que*)
- **BEFORE COMPUTERS:** Also defined as (BC*). In a time before everything done in a radio station was automated by computer including the disc jockeys which are now

called 'Voice-over-persons,' OR 'Voice Trackers.' (*See Engineer; he is only thing left not automated.*)

- **BROADCAST:** To cast broadly, or spread widely what you say. *(see program)*
- **BROADCASTING:** To a DJ can mean; 'casting for a broad!' You can also hear them saying 'broad-chasing,'
- **CART:** (1) BC* (see Before Computers) something to which either recorded music or commercials are transferred to for broadcast. (2) Replaced turntable. (See Turntable) (3) Most of the time referred to by the DJ's as ..." where is that $#&@%$ cart!
- **CART MACHINE:** Device that plays the carts. (*See cart, see if you dare ... the engineer!*)
- **COMMERCIAL:** (1) The thirty or sixty seconds of words gathered together to convince you to buy just what you don't need at the moment. (2) Words that sometime allow the DJ to buy baby a new pair of shoes. (3) Words that make the radio Salesperson that sold the commercial rich! (See Spot. See Spot run! No just kidding! Spot run, is in reality this complex formula; (*X times how many commercials run on the air* = *equals TOTAL $$$*)
- **COMMUNICATE:** (1) What the DJ <u>hopefully</u> does. (2) What the management <u>insist</u> the DJ does ... or he is <u>FIRED!</u>
- **COMPUTER:** Oh, come on ... *MUST* we explain this to anyone? (*If so send them to engineer who will say, "Let me show you all this weird stuff in this box!"*)
- **CONTEST:** Run to attract (1) listeners (2) ratings (3) to make listeners lives complicated. (4) To turn disc jockey's minds into mounds of jelly. (*see ratings*) (*see promotion*)

- **CONTROL ROOM:** (1) where the DJ's program originated inside the radio station BC* (2) Now, on rare occasions in today's radio broadcast it originates from at the radio station. (3) Where even sometimes today a live DJ 'controls all ... or (*please see ratings*)
- **CUE/QUE:** (1) Used by DJ's to get everything ready to go on the air, if live DJ is used. If not ... (See AC*) for your guess is as good as mine and the engineers doesn't count.
- **DEREGULATE:** New rules for radio stations to replace the rules that replaces the other rules that were amended from the first draft of the original rules set up by the Federalizes of the FCC. (*Huh?*)(*See Federal Communication Commission*)(*See pay BIG fine!*)
- **DISC:** (1) Same as disk. (2) A phonograph record. (*see disk, see record*)
- **DISK:** MUST we repeat the above crap?
- **DISK JOCKEY:** (1) One who spins records, carts, CD's, tapes, transcriptions, or cassettes, but all that today after AC* they are listed as music wave files, mp3 files. (2) Same is in disc jockey or deejay. (3) DJ for short, not necessarily short DJ's. (*see announcer*) (*See all of the above!*)(Now I'm even confused?)
- **DUMB:** (1) What the DJ thinks about the Program Director. (2) What the Program Director thinks about the Manager. (3) What the Engineer think about ... oh, the hell with it!
- **DUMMY LOAD:** (1) Term of technical talk used by engineer to confuse everyone. (2) What the engineer is after four beers.
- **EARPHONES:** (1) Devices DJ's wear on their ears to help them hear what is on-the-air. (2) After several years of wearing them and listening to LOUD music, DJ calls

them ... *HEARING AIDS!* (3) Also called 'head' phones, or 'can's'. No not bathroom! (see Monitor)

- **ENGINEER:** (We were dreading this!) (1) One who assembles and fixes broadcast stuff. (2) Does not speak English. (3) Is in a world of his own, most of the time. (4) Complex to them is only a word. (5) Usually identified by the four ballpoint pens, two slide rulers and three screwdrivers in left shirt pocket, flashlight clipped on belt along with three cell phones, and two beepers. (6) Guidelines for the creation of the word—'NERD.' (7) The LAST person on earth to say, *"Why is that smoking?"*

- **FEDERAL COMMUNICATIONS COMMISSION:** (1) FCC for short and usually staffed by short government people. (2) A governmental group of employees need we explain anymore? (3) Gives its permission, (only after radio station owners pull their hair out), to make a radio stations employees follow more rules and regulations that you could read about in a year. (4) Authorized to change those rules daily to keep broadcasters on their toes. (5) Has more power than the light company and can pull the plug on any radio broadcast or radio station at the first sign of anything it suspects in wrong. (6) It suspects EVERYTHING! (*See Deregulate, see station manager, see engineer.*) Strangely enough, engineer and FCC can talk to each other!

- **FORECAST:** (1) As in weather. (2) As good a guess as anyone else could make! (*See Fortune Teller!*)

- **FORMATS:** (1) Type of programs on the radio. (2) Some of the time understood by listeners. (3) Sometimes good, sometimes bad. Examples: "Why is that radio station playing all that redneck-hillbilly-country and western-crap?" Or ... "Why is that there radio station playing all that sound alike hip-pity-hopping-teeny-bubble gum-hippy-terrible loud stuff? It's crap!) (see Ratings)

- **FREQUENCY:** (BC*) the place on the radio dial where listeners tuned to hear their favorite DJ. (AC*) Click on something? Click maybe on 'down load'. Then click on listen. Then click on 'background.' (*See engineer if you are really desperate to know what to click!*)

- **GOOD GUY:** (1) Name once used to describe jock/jocks or DJ/and other names. (2) Other name examples, Air Force, Men of the Microphones, Tower of Power People, Radio Rangers, Platter Patrol and other (sic) slick and sick (*AKA also-known-as*) names. (3) To radio station manager, Good Guys, DJ's and other '*AKA'S* were usually referred to as ..."&#$@% *IDIOTS!*"

- **GROOVE:** (1) Scratches on a phonograph record or CD that somehow makes music. (*Engineer? You take responsibility not me!*) (2) Old word used (BC*) by DJ's in sixties and seventies and picked up by listeners. Example: "That's groovy, man!"

- **JOCK:** (1) Same as DJ. (2) Rides the airwaves. (*See DJ, see disc/disk jockey again and again ... gad!*)

- **JOCK LOUNGE:** (1) Where DJ goes after his time on the air, to A: Cry, B: Scream, C: Bang head against wall. (2) Rubber room with padded walls and floors. (3) Has restraining straps if DJ requests them in advance from receptionist at front desk. (4) NEVER admit Engineer to this room, EVER!

- **KILOCYCLE:** (1) A thousand something? (2) changed from Hertz to uh ... and that's not the rent-a-car thing but yet, Lord ... oh, gosh ... (Don't pass go. *Go see Engineer.*)

- **LISTENER:** (1) YOU! (2) What this book is about. (3) What would DJ's do without them!

- **LIVE:** (1) An actual performance to be transmitted as it happens mostly BC*. (2) What the LIVE disc jockey should be or else!
- **LOG:** (BC*) A written guide on paper telling the DJ what spot or commercial to run next. (AC*) Tells the computer what commercial to run next because the DJ is no longer in the radio station, has gone home, or has been terminated.
- **LONGWAVE:** (1) Not a short wave? (*See you know who!*)
- **METHODOLOGY:** (1) Buzz word used by program director to figure out the music and things to do each day to keep him busy. Usually things pasted to a dart board. (2) Shouted by all radio people, "There must be a method to this madness!" (AC*) Even this is slowly replacing the Program Director because computers can understand methodology, can understand—can under—can under—under—understand. (*See research, call engineer again!*)
- **MICROPHONE:** (1) Instrument that converts the mechanical energy of DJ sounds into electronic signals!) (*Good grief, see what happens when you ask the engineer a simple question about a microphone!*)
- **MIKE:** (1) Short for microphone. (2) Name of an engineer I once knew. (*See—"Please don't make me see the engineer again, I'll be good, really!"*)
- **MONITOR:** (1) To listen to what is going out on the air waves. (2) Some DJ's call the engineer a Monitor lizard because he listens so much to the radio signal.
- **MUSIC:** (1) Real reason you turned on the radio, right? (2) You can still get a little of it played in-between loud and long commercials. (3) (BC*) the reason the DJ had a job. (4) (AC*) the reason fewer DJ's are around to play the music. It is a computer no-brainer, so why do

you need so many DJ's when one DJ can be on over a thousand radio stations playing the same music? (*See 'Don't get me started!'*) (*CRITICAL NOTE*) <u>Never</u> allow engineer to <u>*pick*</u> or <u>*play*</u> the music!

- **MUSIC CHART:** List of songs the music director and radio station 'thinks' you want to hear, even if you really don't want to hear them. (*see Music Director*) (*see Request/Music*)

- **MUSIC DIRECTOR:** (1) Person who using methodology, music charts and voodoo, tries to cram two hundred new songs a week into only seven new positions that are available for broadcast. (2) Usual traits include ... lack of decision making process, thus ask the program director who ask the ... and so on. (*see methodology, see music pick sheets, see payola*)

- **MUSIC PICK SHEET:** (1) Mostly published and read by the music and radio industry. Will tell everyone what to play, right or wrong. (2) Sometimes called 'trade' sheets because they 'may trade favors' which could cause FCC to put DJ on top of its pick list, *TO PICK UP AND PUT IN JAIL!*

- **MUSIC PROMOTER:** (1) Also called 'Rep' or record promoter. (2) Tells radio what his company pays him to say to play. (3) In some cases used to actually PAY DJ to play their songs! Long BC*. A *HUGE* NO NO today! (*See Payola. See FCC, and see DJ go to jail!*)

- **MUSIC REQUEST:** (1) What you (listener) want to hear at least twenty times in a row, every day. (2) What causes insanity, feebleness and old age in DJ's by the time they are twenty-two!

- **NEWSMAN:** (1) "We want just the facts, ma'am." (2) Knows all the gossip and to hear news people tell it they out investigates the police, FBI, CIA, Homeland Security and Sherlock Holmes. (3) Given the right amount of time, (usually thirty seconds), can tell his listeners what color panties you are wearing right now! (4) Is heard running around the newsroom yelling, "Stop the press!" and "Bulletin! Bulletin!"

- **NEWSROOM:** (1) Where the news person hides out most of the day, gathering the news stories from the newspaper to read on the air. (2) Room full of police scanners that modulate waves of static all day long. (3) Has computer to write the news on that somehow the letter, 'h' and 'a' don't work.

- **NUMBER ONE SONG:** (1) The most popular song according to whoever is in charge this week.

- **NUMBER TWO SONG:** (2) Follows number one. (2) Is a *LONG, VERY LONG SONG* a disc jockey plays when he has to go to the bathroom! (*See engineer for other numbers, but watch out if he gets his slide ruler out.*)

- **OLDIE:** (1) Burned out music you never want to hear again. (2) Burned out DJ you never want to hear again. (3) All burned out radio parts the engineer can't explain. Example; "Well, it was just an oldie part."

- **ON-THE-AIR:** "The microphone is turned on, say something, stupid!"

- **POT:** (1) A volume control the DJ uses to control level of sound. (2) And you thought it was something illegal? (See engineer. He is the only one that can really spell the long version of pot. Uh potent-u-om-meter, potentenimator ... OR something similar that!)

- **PROMOTION:** Same as a contest. (see ratings)

- **PLATTER:** (1) Old term to describe records. (2) You are ancient if you remember term or a recording group of singers called the Platters!

- **PROGRAM:** (1) Simply put that stuff you listen to on the radio. (2) A list of acts, speeches, musical pieces, that makes up show biz. (3) (AC*) thought of as something written in long lines of letters that make no sense to anyone but another computer.
- **PROGRAM DIRECTOR:** (1) Not so simply put but usually necessary to guard the door to keep DJ's in the control room. (2) First fired if ratings dip, slip or drop. (*see ratings*)
- **PSA:** (1) Short for 'Public Service Announcement.' (2) A necessary evil. Must run as many per week or month or yearly as required by government. (3) Usually boring. (4) Usually run late at night. (*see ratings, see FCC*)
- **RADIO:** (1) Do we really have to explain? (2) A box with electronic stuff in it that listeners hear disc jockeys talking through. (3) What this book is about. (*See, no, don't, do not, even search for the engineers door! You will never return!*)
- **RADIO STATION:** (1) Building similar in design to a mental institution. (2) Where what few DJ's that are left today play and have breakdowns. (2) Also a pit full of snakes, worms and vampires!
- **RATINGS:** (1) An independent survey and evaluation of how good, or not good a DJ show is. (2) The dirtiest, foulest, word you could ever use in a conversation with any radio person. (3) More important than a DJ's *PAYCHECK*, if he wishes to remain employed. (*See program director and all other crybabies!*)
- **RECEPTIONIST:** (1) Poor lady that has to answer all incoming calls and tell you the boss is in conference. (2) Truly, the only person that really runs the radio station.
- **REMOTE:** (1) Broadcast outside of radio station. (*See broadcast.*)

- **REQUEST LINES:** (1) Do we really have to tell you about this? We *COULD* make you see the engineer! (2) Line you really want to call to talk to the DJ about a song request. (3) Line that DJ usually has *ON HOLD* through most of his show. (*See DJ who has a request of where the engineer could stick the telephone.*)
- **SHORTWAVE:** Not a long one. (*See you know who!*)
- **STATION MANAGER:** (1) sometimes called, "GENERAL" as a rank like head-honcho. (2) Person responsible for delegating blame if something goes wrong. (3) Takes credit if something goes right! (4) For some strange reason wants to really be the Program Director? (5) Only at radio station for ten minutes in the morning then usually found at the Country Club, golf course or on Yacht! (*If he has to see the engineer, mumbles like he understands everything, shakes the engineers hand and says, "Good work!"*) (6) Last thing you will always hear a station manager say, *"I'm late for a big meeting, sorry, gotta go."*
- **SALES PERSON:** (1) is amazing at convincing sane business person to buy *SECONDS OF AIR!* (2) Makes more money than anyone at radio station. (3) Last fired if anything goes wrong because *THEY* bring in the *GREEN STUFF* according to them ... not the disc jockeys! (4) Can usually be found at the same places as Station or General Manager's. (5) Motto. *"THE CLIENT IS ALWAYS RIGHT and so is the GENERAL MANAGER!"* (*Engineer? They have no idea who or what an engineer is?*)
- **SOUND:** (1) Depends on what you define as something like a noise. (*Again ... see Engineer; He can show you some dirty pictures of what sound looks like. Just don't stand too close to him!*)

- **SPOT:** (1) Same as commercial. (2) Easier for DJ to spell and say. *Example; "Damn, I ran a hundred spots on the air today!"*
- **STAX-OF-WAX:** If you remember this term you were around when the phonograph was invented!
- **STEREO:** (1) Sounds very good. (2) It is mostly on FM, which you might remember is different than AM. Or to more precisely quote the engineers example; *"Put one finger in ear, what you hear is AM radio. Now, leave both ears unstopped. Hey, dude ... that's STEREO! (Aren't your sorry now you just had to ask the engineer to explain?)*
- **STICK:** (1) A tall tower or pole that the broadcast program jumps off of and floats in the air until it reaches your radio. *(You know who said that!)*
- **TALK SHOW:** (1) Yak, yak! Blankly blank this and that and so on!
- **TRANSMITTER:** (1) Apparatus that transmits signals, sound waves and such. (2) Usually found in same remote building where the engineer hides out and sleeps. *(See big Poo-Ba of things that hum or glow in the dark or Darth Vader to understand how it operates.)*
- **TURNTABLE:** (1) Round table that turns around and around and was used to play recorded records of music and stuff. (BC*) Long before, most people in broadcasting have never seen a turntable. Just like many have never seen a real disc jockey, same applies to turntable!
- **VOLUME CONTROL:** (1) Wait a moment I can't hear you! (2) used by kids to turn up so loud it shatters windows and gives your cat a heart attack. *(See Pot. No, not smoke pot ... see, see pot definition. Can't you hear me?)*

- **WATTS:** (1) The power of a broadcast signal. (What?) (2) A ghetto in LA. (Former Secretary of Interior that disliked rock music. (4) "Watts happen' man!"
- **X-MITTER:** (1) Short for transmitter. (2) The way the word is pronounced by engineer who had his teeth knocked out by *frustrated* reader of this book!)
- **ZOO:** (1) Glassed in room a disc jockey works. (2) Inside of engineer's office, *DO NOT FEED. (See control room.)*

A SPECIAL NOTICE About: "The DJ's Diaries!"

A WARNING

**"If you've <u>ever</u> turned on a radio … and called a DJ … this book might be about …
YOU!"**

Volume one is a direct result of conversations and incidents that have taken place between disc jockeys and their listeners.

"It is **not** just stories recalling my sixy-plus years behind the microphone dealing with listeners (you) in front of the radio, but the recollections from hundreds' of DJ's who recounted these stories from their own, **"DJ Diaries."**

Let me clear something up about DJ's.

We 'talk shop' the same as you do about your work. We exchange stories about our everyday dealings with our listeners and sometime our fans—YOU!

From that came the years of condensing notes about those *'Remarkable'* conversations.

I think I can safely say that DJ's are no different than you when it comes to gossiping 'locker room stories'! Reality is … disc jockeys are BETTER at embellishing the facts! Thus confirming fact or fiction was not always possible due to the nature of some of the involvements. We have changed names, locations and radio station call letters to protect those we write about.

The Reasons will become obvious!

It must be noted—Most of the stories herein **do not represent most listeners, nor do all DJ's** experience what are contained on the pages of this book.

Statically, only about one percent of you that ever listen to a radio will ever call or write a DJ in your lifetime! An even smaller percent of these DJ's and listeners make up the stories that were gathered for this the first volume. (See a special invitation to become a part of volume three at the end of this book)

"Radio's Remarkable Listeners; The DJ Diaries" does clarify a few crazies--

Listeners do it with their ears!
Disk Jockeys do it with their mouths!
And without (YOU) the listeners!
There would be no (US) the disk jockeys!

If you are a DJ or Listener and would like to contact me and tell me your stories please use my web site;

davedonahue.net

thanks